# Bipolar Mood Journal

## Mastering mood disorders one day at a time.

D1521675

Becka's Best Publishing

Bipolar Mood and Symptom Tracker Journal for people with mood disorders like Bipolar I. & II., Depression, and Anxiety. This journal is designed to track your daily moods, habits, goals, and practice self-care in a healthy way. This journal is great way to document your health to share with your doctor to guarantee the best care.

Becka's Best Publishing

# Contents

Becka's Best Publishing

# About Bi-Polar

Do you have unexplainable highs and lows that cycle on and off without your control? Congratulations, you could have Bipolar Disorder. The difference between Bipolar and "regular seasons of life" are medically defined by 3 factors; the severity of the episodes, the frequency of the episodes, and presence of a family history.

There are 4 basic types of Bipolar:

I.      Defined as severe Manic Episodes that last at least 7 days, followed by at least 2 weeks of depression, with the potential of symptoms of psychosis, usually results in hospitalization.

II.      Defined as Hypomanic Episode that lasts at least 4 days usually followed by a prolonged depressive episode

III.      Also called Cyclothymic Disorder is defined as repeated cycling of hypomanic and depressive-like symptoms over a two-year period.

IV.      Defined as any bipolar symptoms that don't match the severity as the disorders described above.

Becka's Best Publishing

But Bipolar often goes misdiagnosed, especially type II. Nobody wants to go to the doctor and tell them about when they are feeling good, so they end up with a depression diagnosis. The problem with this is the wrong medication can cause major manic and depressive swings which can be more detrimental than helpful.

In addition to massive swings, people with Bipolar are susceptible to mixed states, in which an individual experiences both manic and depressive symptoms.

Recording your moods, medications, external factors, aided by regular and consistent self-reflections, you can begin to understand and master your Bipolar Disorder.

Typical Bipolar treatments include medication of some form, therapy (cognitive and psychotherapy), and healthier daily habits. Bipolar will never be cured, but it can be managed – if you are willing to actively take care of yourself.

## Typical Symptoms

Mania: Feeling "high", elated, euphoric, inflated self-esteem, motivated, talking fast, feeling jumpy or wired, feeling agitated or easily irritated, not sleeping well, hypersexuality

Depressive: feeling down, sad, tired, fatigued, sleepy, slow, thinking slower, the future feels bleak, having trouble concentrating, sleeping too much, eating more/less than usual, self-medicating

Becka's Best Publishing

# Safety Plan

## Why do I need a Safety Plan?

Bipolar, in all its forms, and mood disorders like it are recurring. Each full-blown episode of depression or mania will get more intense and damaging over time. We can prevent that with help, support and a safety plan in place. Please fill out the next few pages of this journal when you are in a relatively good place.

A Bipolar Safety Plan should be shared with key friends and family. It details stressors, things that cause episodes, symptoms of episodes, ways to handle the symptoms and behaviors, and when to get help.

Review this journal with your support team. Tell them about your goals and what you plan to do to achieve them. Share how you are feeling with them; they might be able to tell you when you are experiencing an episode more than you can identify them.

If you are new to learning your bipolar and knowing exactly what it looks like when it is affecting you, add your unique symptoms as you learn about them. This will help you identify and begin to see those symptoms, actions, and behaviors when they happen.

# Who Are You?

Name: _____

DOB: _____

Address:

_____

Phone: _____

E-Mail:

_____

Draw Yourself!

**Likes:** (Colors, Foods, Sports, Activities, Hobbies)

_____

_____

**Dislikes:** (Triggers, Events, Holidays, People)

_____

_____

**General Mood:** (How do you feel right now? Manic, Depressed, Anxious, Mixed)

_____

_____

Becka's Best Publishing

# My Symptoms:

Mania:_____
_____

Depression:_____
_____

Mixed:_____
_____

Stressors: _____
_____
_____

Notes: _____
_____
_____
_____
_____

Becka's Best Publishing

# My Support

Without loyal friends and family to help us when we cannot help ourselves, many of us wouldn't still be here today. I agree to let any of the people listed below to use their best judgement to get me whatever help they deem necessary.

## Family/Friends

1.

2.

3.

4.

5.

## Ways in which my Family/Friends can help me:

1)

2)

3)

4)

5)

Becka's Best Publishing

# Medical Consult

Diagnosis: _____

Date of Diagnosis: _____

Medication(s): _____

_____

_____

_____

Therapist: _____Phone: _____

Primary Doctor: _____Phone: _____

Nurse: _____ Phone: _____

Pharmacy: _____Phone: _____

Nearest ER: _____Phone: _____

Emergency Contacts:

Name: _____ Phone: _____

Name: _____ Phone: _____

Name: _____ Phone: _____

Becka's Best Publishing

# Appointments

| Date: | Time: | Who: | Where: | Attended: |
|-------|-------|------|--------|-----------|
|       |       |      |        |           |
|       |       |      |        |           |
|       |       |      |        |           |
|       |       |      |        |           |
|       |       |      |        |           |
|       |       |      |        |           |
|       |       |      |        |           |
|       |       |      |        |           |
|       |       |      |        |           |
|       |       |      |        |           |
|       |       |      |        |           |
|       |       |      |        |           |
|       |       |      |        |           |

Becka's Best Publishing

| Date: | Time: | Who: | Where | Attended: |
|-------|-------|------|-------|-----------|
|       |       |      |       |           |
|       |       |      |       |           |
|       |       |      |       |           |
|       |       |      |       |           |
|       |       |      |       |           |
|       |       |      |       |           |
|       |       |      |       |           |
|       |       |      |       |           |
|       |       |      |       |           |
|       |       |      |       |           |
|       |       |      |       |           |
|       |       |      |       |           |
|       |       |      |       |           |

Becka's Best Publishing

# Goal Setting: Qaurterly

Setting goals with Bipolar can be difficult at times because often our mood swings and erratic behavior can set us off-course. This journal is designed to last three months long to keep it short and to-the-point. Having a new journal quarterly and giving you the ability to review your state so frequently will keep you more grounded and on track.

Quarterly goals will help you develop new skills consistently, be more accountable, stick to your morning/nighttime rituals, stay on task, and manage your goals better. Get started below by breaking your goal down into manageable bits. Visualize your goal and what you would have to do to get you closer to where you want to be in 3 months.

## My 3-Month Goal: I want (ex: to be stable and in a healthy relationship with my significant other.)

_____

_____

_____

Name one thing you will do each month to reach that goal.

Month 1: _____

Month 2: _____

Month 3: _____

Month: _____ Year: _____

# What are you doing this month to achieve your goals?

Monthly Goal: _____

Purpose: _____

Morning Routine:_____

_____

_____

Night Routine:_____

_____

_____

Habits you want to change: _____

_____

Mood Goals: _____

_____

Medications (Type/Dosage/ Refill Date): _____

_____

_____

_____

Becka's Best Publishing

# Notes:

_____

_____

_____

_____

_____

_____

_____

_____

_____

_____

_____

_____

_____

_____

_____

_____

_____

_____

_____

Becka's Best Publishing

Month: _____ Year: _____

## What are you doing this month to achieve your goals?

Monthly Goal: _____

Purpose: _____

Morning Routine:_____

_____

_____

Night Routine:_____

_____

_____

Habits you want to change: _____

_____

Mood Goals: _____

_____

Medications (Type/Dosage/ Refill Date): _____

_____

_____

_____

Becka's Best Publishing

# Notes:

Notes: Month: _____ Year: _____

## What are you doing this month to achieve your goals?

Monthly Goal: _____

Purpose: _____

Morning Routine:_____

_____

_____

Night Routine:_____

_____

_____

Habits you want to change: _____

_____

Mood Goals: _____

_____

Medications (Type/Dosage/ Refill Date): _____

_____

_____

_____

Becka's Best Publishing

# Notes:

Becka's Best Publishing

# Qaurterly Goal Review:

After each month review and adjust your goals. What went right? What went wrong? What will you do differently next time?

Month 1: _____

_____

_____

_____

_____

Month 2: _____

_____

_____

_____

_____

Month 3: _____

_____

_____

_____

_____

Becka's Best Publishing

# Weekly Goals

Weekly goals are great for self-reflection, especially because we live our lives week to week. The best way to detect a change in our mood or behavior is to review our week and the goals we completed.

We start by breaking down the week with a basic goal, any appointments we need to attend, a list of tasks needed to be completed, a quick reflection and drawing out your emotional state.

These exercises are designed to keep you focused, on task, and in-tune with your psychological subconscious. Each week of the month features a different emotional landscape to keep it fun, fresh, and creative. No two weeks are alike, let them be unique.

Name some different goals you could accomplish in a 1-week time period:

○           ○

○           ○

○           ○

○           ○

○           ○

○           ○

○           ○

○           ○

Becka's Best Publishing

Week: _____

Weekly Goal:_____

Appointments:_____

To-Do List:                          Self-reflection (How did this week go?
                                     What were some things that influenced your
○                                    mood?)_____

○                                    _____

○                                    _____

○                                    _____

                                     _____

Draw your emotional state in the form of a Garden:

Becka's Best Publishing

Week: _____

Weekly Goal:_____

Appointments:_____

To-Do List:

○

○

○

○

Self-reflection (How did this week go? What were some things that influenced your mood?)_____

_____

_____

_____

_____

Draw your emotional state in the form of a Zoo:

Becka's Best Publishing

Week: _____

Weekly Goal:_____

Appointments:_____

To-Do List:

○

○

○

○

Self-reflection (How did this week go? What were some things that influenced your mood?)_____

_____

_____

_____

_____

Draw your emotional state in the form of the Weather:

Week: _____

Weekly Goal:_____

Appointments:_____

To-Do List:

○

○

○

○

Self-reflection (How did this week go? What were some things that influenced your mood?)_____

_____

_____

_____

_____

Draw your emotional state in the form of a Planetary System:

Becka's Best Publishing

# Week: _____

Weekly Goal:_____

Appointments:_____

To-Do List:

○

○

○

○

Self-reflection (How did this week go?
What were some things that influenced your
mood?)_____

_____

_____

_____

_____

_____

Draw your emotional state in the form of a Garden:

Becka's Best Publishing

Week: _____

Weekly Goal: _____

Appointments: _____

To-Do List:

○

○

○

○

Self-reflection (How did this week go? What were some things that influenced your mood?) _____

_____

_____

_____

_____

Draw your emotional state in the form of a Zoo:

Becka's Best Publishing

Week: _____

Weekly Goal:_____

Appointments:_____

To-Do List:

○

○

○

○

Self-reflection (How did this week go? What were some things that influenced your mood?)_____

_____

_____

_____

_____

_____

Draw your emotional state in the form of the Weather:

Becka's Best Publishing

Week: _____

Weekly Goal:_____

Appointments:_____

To-Do List:

○

○

○

○

Self-reflection (How did this week go? What were some things that influenced your mood?)_____

_____

_____

_____

_____

Draw your emotional state in the form of a Planetary System:

Becka's Best Publishing

Week: _____

Weekly Goal: _____

Appointments: _____

To-Do List:

○

○

○

○

Self-reflection (How did this week go? What were some things that influenced your mood?) _____

_____

_____

_____

_____

Draw your emotional state in the form of a Garden:

Becka's Best Publishing

Week: _____

Weekly Goal:_____

Appointments:_____

To-Do List:

○

○

○

○

Self-reflection (How did this week go? What were some things that influenced your mood?)_____

_____

_____

_____

_____

Draw your emotional state in the form of a Zoo:

Becka's Best Publishing

# Week: _____

Weekly Goal:_____

Appointments:_____

To-Do List:

○

○

○

○

Self-reflection (How did this week go? What were some things that influenced your mood?)_____

_____

_____

_____

_____

Draw your emotional state in the form of the Weather:

Becka's Best Publishing

# Week: _____

Weekly Goal: _____

Appointments: _____

To-Do List:

○ 

○ 

○ 

○ 

Self-reflection (How did this week go?
What were some things that influenced your
mood?) _____

_____

_____

_____

_____

Draw your emotional state in the form of a Planetary System:

Becka's Best Publishing

# Weekly Reflections

Week 1: _____

Week 2: _____

Week 3: _____

Week 4: _____

Week 5: _____

Week 6: _____

Week 7: _____

Week 8: _____

Week 9: _____

Week 10: _____

Week 11: _____

Week 12: _____

Becka's Best Publishing

# Daily Aspirations

The Daily goals of this journal were designed to keep your mental and physical well-being in mind. Medication alone will not "cure" your mood disorder. Strict self-discipline and health management is the best way to consistently manage your condition.

On the Daily journal pages you will be able to track healthy habits, sleep quality —as that can be a major symptom of what Bipolar stage you are in- and chart your moods throughout the day and reflect on the day. There is also plenty of space for extra notes to detail any other symptoms or outside factors that influenced or affected your overall daily mood.

Setting daily goals gives purpose to your day. I believe that is the best way to stay on track, even if you fall off. This journal is not meant to treat you like a broken human who just isn't thinking positively enough, but rather a very real one with dreams and aspirations that you would like to achieve despite your mood condition.

Name some daily habits and behaviors you want to focus on changing:

- ○

- ○

- ○

- ○

- ○

Date: _____ Day: _____ Time: _____

Daily Goal: _____

## To- Do List

- ○
- ○
- ○
- ○

## Daily Habits

- ○ Drink Water
- ○ Personal Hygiene
- ○ Exercise
- ○ Meditate
- ○ Eat a healthy meal

# Sleep:

Quality: _____          Wake-Up; _____

Hours: _____          Bedtime: _____

# Chart your mood throughout the day:

Mood Chart

12:00 AM
9:36 PM
7:12 PM
4:48 PM
2:24 PM
12:00 PM
9:36 AM
7:12 AM
4:48 AM
2:24 AM
12:00 AM

Happy  Motivated  Anxious  Manic  Stable  Sad  Frustrated  Angry  Depressed  Tired

Becka's Best Publishing

# Self- Reflection:

Things you did today to achieve your goals: _____

_____

_____

_____

Things you did today that hindered your goals: _____

_____

_____

_____

Things that went well: _____

_____

_____

_____

Things that could have gone better: _____

_____

_____

_____

Notes: _____

_____

_____

_____

Becka's Best Publishing

Date: _____ Day: _____ Time: _____

Daily Goal: _____

## To- Do List

- ○
- ○
- ○
- ○

## Daily Habits

- ○ Drink Water
- ○ Personal Hygiene
- ○ Exercise
- ○ Meditate
- ○ Eat a healthy meal

# Sleep:

Quality: _____      Wake-Up: _____

Hours: _____      Bedtime: _____

# Chart your mood throughout the day:

### Mood Chart

| | | | | | | | | | |
|---|---|---|---|---|---|---|---|---|---|
| 12:00 AM | | | | | | | | | |
| 9:36 PM | | | | | | | | | |
| 7:12 PM | | | | | | | | | |
| 4:48 PM | | | | | | | | | |
| 2:24 PM | | | | | | | | | |
| 12:00 PM | | | | | | | | | |
| 9:36 AM | | | | | | | | | |
| 7:12 AM | | | | | | | | | |
| 4:48 AM | | | | | | | | | |
| 2:24 AM | | | | | | | | | |
| 12:00 AM | | | | | | | | | |

Happy  Motivated  Anxious  Manic  Stable  Sad  Frustrated  Angry  Depressed  Tired

Becka's Best Publishing

# Self- Reflection:

Things you did today to achieve your goals: _____

_____

_____

_____

Things you did today that hindered your goals: _____

_____

_____

_____

Things that went well: _____

_____

_____

_____

Things that could have gone better: _____

_____

_____

_____

Notes: _____

_____

_____

_____

Becka's Best Publishing

Date: _____ Day: _____ Time: _____

Daily Goal: _____

## To-Do List

- ○
- ○
- ○
- ○

## Daily Habits

- ○ Drink Water
- ○ Personal Hygiene
- ○ Exercise
- ○ Meditate
- ○ Eat a healthy meal

## Sleep:

Quality: _____        Wake-Up: _____

Hours: ____        Bedtime: _____

## Chart your mood throughout the day:

Mood Chart

12:00 AM
9:36 PM
7:12 PM
4:48 PM
2:24 PM
12:00 PM
9:36 AM
7:12 AM
4:48 AM
2:24 AM
12:00 AM

Happy  Motivated  Anxious  Manic  Stable  Sad  Frustrated  Angry  Depressed  Tired

Becka's Best Publishing

# Self- Reflection:

Things you did today to achieve your goals: _____

_____

_____

_____

Things you did today that hindered your goals: _____

_____

_____

_____

Things that went well: _____

_____

_____

_____

Things that could have gone better: _____

_____

_____

_____

Notes: _____

_____

_____

_____

Becka's Best Publishing

# Date: _____ Day: _____ Time: _____

## Daily Goal: _____

## To- Do List

- ○
- ○
- ○
- ○

## Daily Habits

- ○ Drink Water
- ○ Personal Hygiene
- ○ Exercise
- ○ Meditate
- ○ Eat a healthy meal

## Sleep:

Quality: _____          Wake-Up: _____

Hours: _____          Bedtime: _____

## Chart your mood throughout the day:

Mood Chart

| | |
|---|---|
| 12:00 AM | |
| 9:36 PM | |
| 7:12 PM | |
| 4:48 PM | |
| 2:24 PM | |
| 12:00 PM | |
| 9:36 AM | |
| 7:12 AM | |
| 4:48 AM | |
| 2:24 AM | |
| 12:00 AM | |

Happy  Motivated  Anxious  Manic  Stable  Sad  Frustrated  Angry  Depressed  Tired

Becka's Best Publishing

# Self- Reflection:

Things you did today to achieve your goals: _____

_____

_____

_____

Things you did today that hindered your goals: _____

_____

_____

_____

Things that went well: _____

_____

_____

_____

Things that could have gone better: _____

_____

_____

_____

Notes: _____

_____

_____

_____

Becka's Best Publishing

Date: _____ Day: _____ Time: _____

Daily Goal: _____

## To- Do List

- ○
- ○
- ○
- ○

## Daily Habits

- ○ Drink Water
- ○ Personal Hygiene
- ○ Exercise
- ○ Meditate
- ○ Eat a healthy meal

## Sleep:

Quality: _____          Wake-Up: _____

Hours: _____          Bedtime: _____

## Chart your mood throughout the day:

Mood Chart

12:00 AM
9:36 PM
7:12 PM
4:48 PM
2:24 PM
12:00 PM
9:36 AM
7:12 AM
4:48 AM
2:24 AM
12:00 AM

Happy   Motivated   Anxious   Manic   Stable   Sad   Frustrated   Angry   Depressed   Tired

Becka's Best Publishing

# Self- Reflection:

Things you did today to achieve your goals: _____

_____

_____

_____

Things you did today that hindered your goals: _____

_____

_____

_____

Things that went well: _____

_____

_____

_____

Things that could have gone better: _____

_____

_____

_____

Notes: _____

_____

_____

_____

Becka's Best Publishing

Date: _____ Day: _____ Time: _____

Daily Goal: _____

## To- Do List

- ○
- ○
- ○
- ○

## Daily Habits

- ○ Drink Water
- ○ Personal Hygiene
- ○ Exercise
- ○ Meditate
- ○ Eat a healthy meal

# Sleep:

Quality: _____          Wake-Up: _____

Hours: ____              Bedtime: _____

# Chart your mood throughout the day:

Mood Chart

| 12:00 AM |
| 9:36 PM |
| 7:12 PM |
| 4:48 PM |
| 2:24 PM |
| 12:00 PM |
| 9:36 AM |
| 7:12 AM |
| 4:48 AM |
| 2:24 AM |
| 12:00 AM |

Happy   Motivated   Anxious   Manic   Stable   Sad   Frustrated   Angry   Depressed   Tired

Becka's Best Publishing

# Self- Reflection:

Things you did today to achieve your goals: _____

_____

_____

_____

Things you did today that hindered your goals: _____

_____

_____

_____

Things that went well: _____

_____

_____

_____

Things that could have gone better: _____

_____

_____

_____

Notes: _____

_____

_____

_____

Becka's Best Publishing

Date: _____ Day: _____ Time: _____

Daily Goal: _____

## To- Do List

- ○
- ○
- ○
- ○

## Daily Habits

- ○ Drink Water
- ○ Personal Hygiene
- ○ Exercise
- ○ Meditate
- ○ Eat a healthy meal

# Sleep:

Quality: _____       Wake-Up: _____

Hours: ____       Bedtime: _____

# Chart your mood throughout the day:

Mood Chart

| 12:00 AM |
| 9:36 PM |
| 7:12 PM |
| 4:48 PM |
| 2:24 PM |
| 12:00 PM |
| 9:36 AM |
| 7:12 AM |
| 4:48 AM |
| 2:24 AM |
| 12:00 AM |

Happy  Motivated  Anxious  Manic  Stable  Sad  Frustrated  Angry  Depressed  Tired

Becka's Best Publishing

# Self- Reflection:

Things you did today to achieve your goals: _____

_____

_____

_____

Things you did today that hindered your goals: _____

_____

_____

_____

Things that went well: _____

_____

_____

_____

Things that could have gone better: _____

_____

_____

_____

Notes: _____

_____

_____

_____

Becka's Best Publishing

Date: _____ Day: _____ Time: _____

Daily Goal: _____

## To- Do List

○

○

○

○

## Daily Habits

○ Drink Water

○ Personal Hygiene

○ Exercise

○ Meditate

○ Eat a healthy meal

# Sleep:

Quality: _____          Wake-Up: _____

Hours: _____          Bedtime: _____

# Chart your mood throughout the day:

### Mood Chart

| | Happy | Motivated | Anxious | Manic | Stable | Sad | Frustrated | Angry | Depressed | Tired |
|---|---|---|---|---|---|---|---|---|---|---|
| 12:00 AM | | | | | | | | | | |
| 9:36 PM | | | | | | | | | | |
| 7:12 PM | | | | | | | | | | |
| 4:48 PM | | | | | | | | | | |
| 2:24 PM | | | | | | | | | | |
| 12:00 PM | | | | | | | | | | |
| 9:36 AM | | | | | | | | | | |
| 7:12 AM | | | | | | | | | | |
| 4:48 AM | | | | | | | | | | |
| 2:24 AM | | | | | | | | | | |
| 12:00 AM | | | | | | | | | | |

Becka's Best Publishing

# Self- Reflection:

Things you did today to achieve your goals: _____

_____

_____

_____

Things you did today that hindered your goals: _____

_____

_____

_____

Things that went well: _____

_____

_____

_____

Things that could have gone better: _____

_____

_____

_____

Notes: _____

_____

_____

_____

Becka's Best Publishing

# Date: _____ Day: _____ Time: _____

# Daily Goal: _____

## To- Do List

○

○

○

○

## Daily Habits

○ Drink Water

○ Personal Hygiene

○ Exercise

○ Meditate

○ Eat a healthy meal

# Sleep:

Quality: _____

Wake-Up: _____

Hours: _____

Bedtime: _____

# Chart your mood throughout the day:

Mood Chart

| 12:00 AM |
| 9:36 PM |
| 7:12 PM |
| 4:48 PM |
| 2:24 PM |
| 12:00 PM |
| 9:36 AM |
| 7:12 AM |
| 4:48 AM |
| 2:24 AM |
| 12:00 AM |

Happy  Motivated  Anxious  Manic  Stable  Sad  Frustrated  Angry  Depressed  Tired

Becka's Best Publishing

# Self- Reflection:

Things you did today to achieve your goals: _____

_____

_____

_____

Things you did today that hindered your goals: _____

_____

_____

_____

Things that went well: _____

_____

_____

_____

Things that could have gone better: _____

_____

_____

_____

Notes: _____

_____

_____

_____

Becka's Best Publishing

Date: _____ Day: _____ Time: _____

Daily Goal: _____

## To- Do List

- ○
- ○
- ○
- ○

## Daily Habits

- ○ Drink Water
- ○ Personal Hygiene
- ○ Exercise
- ○ Meditate
- ○ Eat a healthy meal

# Sleep:

Quality: _____          Wake-Up: _____

Hours: _____          Bedtime: _____

# Chart your mood throughout the day:

Mood Chart

| | |
|---|---|
| 12:00 AM | |
| 9:36 PM | |
| 7:12 PM | |
| 4:48 PM | |
| 2:24 PM | |
| 12:00 PM | |
| 9:36 AM | |
| 7:12 AM | |
| 4:48 AM | |
| 2:24 AM | |
| 12:00 AM | |

Happy   Motivated   Anxious   Manic   Stable   Sad   Frustrated   Angry   Depressed   Tired

Becka's Best Publishing

# Self- Reflection:

Things you did today to achieve your goals: _____

_____

_____

_____

Things you did today that hindered your goals: _____

_____

_____

_____

Things that went well: _____

_____

_____

_____

Things that could have gone better: _____

_____

_____

_____

Notes: _____

_____

_____

_____

Becka's Best Publishing

Date: _____ Day: _____ Time: _____

Daily Goal: _____

## To- Do List

- ○
- ○
- ○
- ○

## Daily Habits

- ○ Drink Water
- ○ Personal Hygiene
- ○ Exercise
- ○ Meditate
- ○ Eat a healthy meal

## Sleep:

Quality: _____          Wake-Up: _____

Hours: _____          Bedtime: _____

## Chart your mood throughout the day:

Mood Chart

| | |
|---|---|
| 12:00 AM | |
| 9:36 PM | |
| 7:12 PM | |
| 4:48 PM | |
| 2:24 PM | |
| 12:00 PM | |
| 9:36 AM | |
| 7:12 AM | |
| 4:48 AM | |
| 2:24 AM | |
| 12:00 AM | |

Happy  Motivated  Anxious  Manic  Stable  Sad  Frustrated  Angry  Depressed  Tired

Becka's Best Publishing

# Self-Reflection:

Things you did today to achieve your goals: _____

_____

_____

_____

Things you did today that hindered your goals: _____

_____

_____

_____

Things that went well: _____

_____

_____

_____

Things that could have gone better: _____

_____

_____

_____

Notes: _____

_____

_____

_____

Becka's Best Publishing

Date: _____ Day: _____ Time: _____

Daily Goal: _____

## To- Do List

- ○
- ○
- ○
- ○

## Daily Habits

- ○ Drink Water
- ○ Personal Hygiene
- ○ Exercise
- ○ Meditate
- ○ Eat a healthy meal

## Sleep:

Quality: _____          Wake-Up: _____

Hours: _____          Bedtime: _____

## Chart your mood throughout the day:

Mood Chart

12:00 AM
9:36 PM
7:12 PM
4:48 PM
2:24 PM
12:00 PM
9:36 AM
7:12 AM
4:48 AM
2:24 AM
12:00 AM

Happy  Motivated  Anxious  Manic  Stable  Sad  Frustrated  Angry  Depressed  Tired

Becka's Best Publishing

# Self- Reflection:

Things you did today to achieve your goals: _____

_____

_____

_____

Things you did today that hindered your goals: _____

_____

_____

_____

Things that went well: _____

_____

_____

_____

Things that could have gone better: _____

_____

_____

_____

Notes: _____

_____

_____

_____

Becka's Best Publishing

Date: _____ Day: _____ Time: _____

Daily Goal: _____

## To- Do List

○

○

○

○

## Daily Habits

○ Drink Water

○ Personal Hygiene

○ Exercise

○ Meditate

○ Eat a healthy meal

# Sleep:

Quality: _____        Wake-Up: _____

Hours: _____           Bedtime: _____

# Chart your mood throughout the day:

Mood Chart

| 12:00 AM |
| 9:36 PM |
| 7:12 PM |
| 4:48 PM |
| 2:24 PM |
| 12:00 PM |
| 9:36 AM |
| 7:12 AM |
| 4:48 AM |
| 2:24 AM |
| 12:00 AM |

Happy  Motivated  Anxious  Manic  Stable  Sad  Frustrated  Angry  Depressed  Tired

Becka's Best Publishing

# Self- Reflection:

Things you did today to achieve your goals: _____
_____
_____
_____

Things you did today that hindered your goals: _____
_____
_____
_____

Things that went well: _____
_____
_____
_____

Things that could have gone better: _____
_____
_____
_____

Notes: _____
_____
_____
_____

Becka's Best Publishing

Date: _____ Day: _____ Time: _____

Daily Goal: _____

## To- Do List

- ○
- ○
- ○
- ○

## Daily Habits

- ○ Drink Water
- ○ Personal Hygiene
- ○ Exercise
- ○ Meditate
- ○ Eat a healthy meal

# Sleep:

Quality: _____          Wake-Up: _____

Hours: ____          Bedtime: _____

# Chart your mood throughout the day:

Mood Chart

```
12:00 AM
 9:36 PM
 7:12 PM
 4:48 PM
 2:24 PM
12:00 PM
 9:36 AM
 7:12 AM
 4:48 AM
 2:24 AM
12:00 AM
         Happy  Motivated  Anxious  Manic  Stable  Sad  Frustrated  Angry  Depressed  Tired
```

Becka's Best Publishing

# Self- Reflection:

Things you did today to achieve your goals: _____

_____

_____

_____

Things you did today that hindered your goals: _____

_____

_____

_____

Things that went well: _____

_____

_____

_____

Things that could have gone better: _____

_____

_____

_____

Notes: _____

_____

_____

_____

Becka's Best Publishing

Date: _____ Day: _____ Time: _____

Daily Goal: _____

## To- Do List

- ○
- ○
- ○
- ○

## Daily Habits

- ○ Drink Water
- ○ Personal Hygiene
- ○ Exercise
- ○ Meditate
- ○ Eat a healthy meal

# Sleep:

Quality: _____        Wake-Up: _____

Hours: _____        Bedtime: _____

# Chart your mood throughout the day:

Mood Chart

| | |
|---|---|
| 12:00 AM | |
| 9:36 PM | |
| 7:12 PM | |
| 4:48 PM | |
| 2:24 PM | |
| 12:00 PM | |
| 9:36 AM | |
| 7:12 AM | |
| 4:48 AM | |
| 2:24 AM | |
| 12:00 AM | |

Happy    Motivated    Anxious    Manic    Stable    Sad    Frustrated    Angry    Depressed    Tired

Becka's Best Publishing

# Self- Reflection:

Things you did today to achieve your goals: _____

_____

_____

_____

Things you did today that hindered your goals: _____

_____

_____

_____

Things that went well: _____

_____

_____

_____

Things that could have gone better: _____

_____

_____

_____

Notes: _____

_____

_____

_____

Becka's Best Publishing

Date: _____ Day: _____ Time: _____

Daily Goal: _____

## To- Do List

- ○
- ○
- ○
- ○

## Daily Habits

- ○ Drink Water
- ○ Personal Hygiene
- ○ Exercise
- ○ Meditate
- ○ Eat a healthy meal

# Sleep:

Quality: _____        Wake-Up: _____

Hours: _____        Bedtime: _____

# Chart your mood throughout the day:

Mood Chart

| 12:00 AM |
| 9:36 PM |
| 7:12 PM |
| 4:48 PM |
| 2:24 PM |
| 12:00 PM |
| 9:36 AM |
| 7:12 AM |
| 4:48 AM |
| 2:24 AM |
| 12:00 AM |

Happy  Motivated  Anxious  Manic  Stable  Sad  Frustrated  Angry  Depressed  Tired

Becka's Best Publishing

# Self- Reflection:

Things you did today to achieve your goals: _____

_____

_____

_____

Things you did today that hindered your goals: _____

_____

_____

_____

Things that went well: _____

_____

_____

_____

Things that could have gone better: _____

_____

_____

_____

Notes: _____

_____

_____

_____

Becka's Best Publishing

Date: _____ Day: _____ Time: _____

Daily Goal: _____

To- Do List

- ○
- ○
- ○
- ○

Daily Habits

- ○ Drink Water
- ○ Personal Hygiene
- ○ Exercise
- ○ Meditate
- ○ Eat a healthy meal

Sleep:

Quality: _____     Wake-Up: _____

Hours: ____     Bedtime: _____

## Chart your mood throughout the day:

Mood Chart

| | Happy | Motivated | Anxious | Manic | Stable | Sad | Frustrated | Angry | Depressed | Tired |
|---|---|---|---|---|---|---|---|---|---|---|
| 12:00 AM | | | | | | | | | | |
| 9:36 PM | | | | | | | | | | |
| 7:12 PM | | | | | | | | | | |
| 4:48 PM | | | | | | | | | | |
| 2:24 PM | | | | | | | | | | |
| 12:00 PM | | | | | | | | | | |
| 9:36 AM | | | | | | | | | | |
| 7:12 AM | | | | | | | | | | |
| 4:48 AM | | | | | | | | | | |
| 2:24 AM | | | | | | | | | | |
| 12:00 AM | | | | | | | | | | |

Becka's Best Publishing

# Self- Reflection:

Things you did today to achieve your goals: _____

_____

_____

_____

Things you did today that hindered your goals: _____

_____

_____

_____

Things that went well: _____

_____

_____

_____

Things that could have gone better: _____

_____

_____

_____

Notes: _____

_____

_____

_____

Becka's Best Publishing

Date: _____ Day: _____ Time: _____

Daily Goal: _____

## To- Do List

- ○
- ○
- ○
- ○

## Daily Habits

- ○ Drink Water
- ○ Personal Hygiene
- ○ Exercise
- ○ Meditate
- ○ Eat a healthy meal

## Sleep:

Quality: _____          Wake-Up: _____

Hours: _____          Bedtime: _____

## Chart your mood throughout the day:

Mood Chart

12:00 AM
9:36 PM
7:12 PM
4:48 PM
2:24 PM
12:00 PM
9:36 AM
7:12 AM
4:48 AM
2:24 AM
12:00 AM

Happy   Motivated   Anxious   Manic   Stable   Sad   Frustrated   Angry   Depressed   Tired

Becka's Best Publishing

# Self- Reflection:

Things you did today to achieve your goals: _____

_____

_____

_____

Things you did today that hindered your goals: _____

_____

_____

_____

Things that went well: _____

_____

_____

_____

Things that could have gone better: _____

_____

_____

_____

Notes: _____

_____

_____

_____

Becka's Best Publishing

Date: _____ Day: _____ Time: _____

Daily Goal: _____

## To- Do List

- ○
- ○
- ○
- ○

## Daily Habits

- ○ Drink Water
- ○ Personal Hygiene
- ○ Exercise
- ○ Meditate
- ○ Eat a healthy meal

# Sleep:

Quality: _____          Wake-Up: _____

Hours: _____          Bedtime: _____

# Chart your mood throughout the day:

Mood Chart

| | 12:00 AM |
| 9:36 PM |
| 7:12 PM |
| 4:48 PM |
| 2:24 PM |
| 12:00 PM |
| 9:36 AM |
| 7:12 AM |
| 4:48 AM |
| 2:24 AM |
| 12:00 AM |

Happy  Motivated  Anxious  Manic  Stable  Sad  Frustrated  Angry  Depressed  Tired

Becka's Best Publishing

# Self- Reflection:

Things you did today to achieve your goals: _____

_____

_____

_____

Things you did today that hindered your goals: _____

_____

_____

_____

Things that went well: _____

_____

_____

_____

Things that could have gone better: _____

_____

_____

_____

Notes: _____

_____

_____

_____

Becka's Best Publishing

Date: _____ Day: _____ Time: _____

Daily Goal: _____

To- Do List                          Daily Habits

○                                    ○   Drink Water

                                     ○   Personal Hygiene
○
                                     ○   Exercise

○                                    ○   Meditate

                                     ○   Eat a healthy meal
○

## Sleep:

Quality: _____         Wake-Up: _____

Hours: ____              Bedtime: _____

## Chart your mood throughout the day:

Mood Chart

|  | |
|---|---|
| 12:00 AM | |
| 9:36 PM | |
| 7:12 PM | |
| 4:48 PM | |
| 2:24 PM | |
| 12:00 PM | |
| 9:36 AM | |
| 7:12 AM | |
| 4:48 AM | |
| 2:24 AM | |
| 12:00 AM | |

Happy   Motivated   Anxious   Manic   Stable   Sad   Frustrated   Angry   Depressed   Tired

Becka's Best Publishing

# Self- Reflection:

Things you did today to achieve your goals: _____

_____

_____

_____

Things you did today that hindered your goals: _____

_____

_____

_____

Things that went well: _____

_____

_____

_____

Things that could have gone better: _____

_____

_____

_____

Notes: _____

_____

_____

_____

Becka's Best Publishing

Date: _____ Day: _____ Time: _____

Daily Goal: _____

## To- Do List

- ○
- ○
- ○
- ○

## Daily Habits

- ○ Drink Water
- ○ Personal Hygiene
- ○ Exercise
- ○ Meditate
- ○ Eat a healthy meal

# Sleep:

Quality: _____          Wake-Up: _____

Hours: ____          Bedtime: _____

# Chart your mood throughout the day:

Mood Chart

| | |
|---|---|
| 12:00 AM | |
| 9:36 PM | |
| 7:12 PM | |
| 4:48 PM | |
| 2:24 PM | |
| 12:00 PM | |
| 9:36 AM | |
| 7:12 AM | |
| 4:48 AM | |
| 2:24 AM | |
| 12:00 AM | |

Happy   Motivated   Anxious   Manic   Stable   Sad   Frustrated   Angry   Depressed   Tired

Becka's Best Publishing

# Self- Reflection:

Things you did today to achieve your goals: _____

_____

_____

_____

Things you did today that hindered your goals: _____

_____

_____

_____

Things that went well: _____

_____

_____

_____

Things that could have gone better: _____

_____

_____

_____

Notes: _____

_____

_____

_____

Becka's Best Publishing

Date: _____ Day: _____ Time: _____

Daily Goal: _____

## To- Do List

o

o

o

o

## Daily Habits

- o Drink Water
- o Personal Hygiene
- o Exercise
- o Meditate
- o Eat a healthy meal

# Sleep:

Quality: _____        Wake-Up: _____

Hours: _____        Bedtime: _____

# Chart your mood throughout the day:

Mood Chart

12:00 AM
9:36 PM
7:12 PM
4:48 PM
2:24 PM
12:00 PM
9:36 AM
7:12 AM
4:48 AM
2:24 AM
12:00 AM

Happy   Motivated   Anxious   Manic   Stable   Sad   Frustrated   Angry   Depressed   Tired

Becka's Best Publishing

# Self- Reflection:

Things you did today to achieve your goals: _____

_____

_____

_____

Things you did today that hindered your goals: _____

_____

_____

_____

Things that went well: _____

_____

_____

_____

Things that could have gone better: _____

_____

_____

_____

Notes: _____

_____

_____

_____

Becka's Best Publishing

Date: _____ Day: _____ Time: _____

Daily Goal: _____

## To- Do List

- ○
- ○
- ○
- ○

## Daily Habits

- ○ Drink Water
- ○ Personal Hygiene
- ○ Exercise
- ○ Meditate
- ○ Eat a healthy meal

# Sleep:

Quality: _____        Wake-Up: _____

Hours: _____        Bedtime: _____

# Chart your mood throughout the day:

Mood Chart

| | Happy | Motivated | Anxious | Manic | Stable | Sad | Frustrated | Angry | Depressed | Tired |
|---|---|---|---|---|---|---|---|---|---|---|
| 12:00 AM | | | | | | | | | | |
| 9:36 PM | | | | | | | | | | |
| 7:12 PM | | | | | | | | | | |
| 4:48 PM | | | | | | | | | | |
| 2:24 PM | | | | | | | | | | |
| 12:00 PM | | | | | | | | | | |
| 9:36 AM | | | | | | | | | | |
| 7:12 AM | | | | | | | | | | |
| 4:48 AM | | | | | | | | | | |
| 2:24 AM | | | | | | | | | | |
| 12:00 AM | | | | | | | | | | |

Becka's Best Publishing

# Self- Reflection:

Things you did today to achieve your goals: _____

_____

_____

_____

Things you did today that hindered your goals: _____

_____

_____

_____

Things that went well: _____

_____

_____

_____

Things that could have gone better: _____

_____

_____

_____

Notes: _____

_____

_____

_____

Becka's Best Publishing

Date: _____ Day: _____ Time: _____

Daily Goal: _____

## To- Do List

- ○
- ○
- ○
- ○

## Daily Habits

- ○  Drink Water
- ○  Personal Hygiene
- ○  Exercise
- ○  Meditate
- ○  Eat a healthy meal

## Sleep:

Quality: _____     Wake-Up: _____

Hours: _____     Bedtime: _____

## Chart your mood throughout the day:

Mood Chart

| 12:00 AM |
| 9:36 PM |
| 7:12 PM |
| 4:48 PM |
| 2:24 PM |
| 12:00 PM |
| 9:36 AM |
| 7:12 AM |
| 4:48 AM |
| 2:24 AM |
| 12:00 AM |

Happy   Motivated   Anxious   Manic   Stable   Sad   Frustrated   Angry   Depressed   Tired

Becka's Best Publishing

# Self- Reflection:

Things you did today to achieve your goals: _____

_____

_____

_____

Things you did today that hindered your goals: _____

_____

_____

_____

Things that went well: _____

_____

_____

_____

Things that could have gone better: _____

_____

_____

_____

Notes: _____

_____

_____

_____

Becka's Best Publishing

Date: _____ Day: _____ Time: _____

Daily Goal: _____

## To- Do List

- ○
- ○
- ○
- ○

## Daily Habits

- ○ Drink Water
- ○ Personal Hygiene
- ○ Exercise
- ○ Meditate
- ○ Eat a healthy meal

# Sleep:

Quality: _____          Wake-Up: _____

Hours: _____              Bedtime: _____

# Chart your mood throughout the day:

Mood Chart

| 12:00 AM |
| 9:36 PM |
| 7:12 PM |
| 4:48 PM |
| 2:24 PM |
| 12:00 PM |
| 9:36 AM |
| 7:12 AM |
| 4:48 AM |
| 2:24 AM |
| 12:00 AM |

Happy  Motivated  Anxious  Manic  Stable  Sad  Frustrated  Angry  Depressed  Tired

Becka's Best Publishing

# Self- Reflection:

Things you did today to achieve your goals: _____

_____

_____

_____

Things you did today that hindered your goals: _____

_____

_____

_____

Things that went well: _____

_____

_____

_____

Things that could have gone better: _____

_____

_____

_____

Notes: _____

_____

_____

_____

Becka's Best Publishing

Date: _____ Day: _____ Time: _____

Daily Goal: _____

To- Do List

- ○
- ○
- ○
- ○

Daily Habits

- ○ Drink Water
- ○ Personal Hygiene
- ○ Exercise
- ○ Meditate
- ○ Eat a healthy meal

## Sleep:

Quality: _____        Wake-Up: _____

Hours: ____        Bedtime: _____

## Chart your mood throughout the day:

Mood Chart

|  | |
|------|--|
| 12:00 AM | |
| 9:36 PM | |
| 7:12 PM | |
| 4:48 PM | |
| 2:24 PM | |
| 12:00 PM | |
| 9:36 AM | |
| 7:12 AM | |
| 4:48 AM | |
| 2:24 AM | |
| 12:00 AM | |

Happy   Motivated   Anxious   Manic   Stable   Sad   Frustrated   Angry   Depressed   Tired

Becka's Best Publishing

# Self- Reflection:

Things you did today to achieve your goals: _____

_____

_____

_____

Things you did today that hindered your goals: _____

_____

_____

_____

Things that went well: _____

_____

_____

_____

Things that could have gone better: _____

_____

_____

_____

Notes: _____

_____

_____

_____

Becka's Best Publishing

Date: _____ Day: _____ Time: _____

Daily Goal: _____

## To-Do List

- ○
- ○
- ○
- ○

## Daily Habits

- ○ Drink Water
- ○ Personal Hygiene
- ○ Exercise
- ○ Meditate
- ○ Eat a healthy meal

# Sleep:

Quality: _____          Wake-Up: _____

Hours: ____              Bedtime: _____

# Chart your mood throughout the day:

Mood Chart

| 12:00 AM |
| 9:36 PM |
| 7:12 PM |
| 4:48 PM |
| 2:24 PM |
| 12:00 PM |
| 9:36 AM |
| 7:12 AM |
| 4:48 AM |
| 2:24 AM |
| 12:00 AM |

Happy  Motivated  Anxious  Manic  Stable  Sad  Frustrated  Angry  Depressed  Tired

Becka's Best Publishing

# Self- Reflection:

Things you did today to achieve your goals: _____

_____

_____

_____

Things you did today that hindered your goals: _____

_____

_____

_____

Things that went well: _____

_____

_____

_____

Things that could have gone better: _____

_____

_____

_____

Notes: _____

_____

_____

_____

Becka's Best Publishing

Date: _____ Day: _____ Time: _____

## Daily Goal: _____

## To- Do List

- ○
- ○
- ○
- ○

## Daily Habits

- ○ Drink Water
- ○ Personal Hygiene
- ○ Exercise
- ○ Meditate
- ○ Eat a healthy meal

# Sleep:

Quality: _____     Wake-Up: _____

Hours: ____     Bedtime: _____

# Chart your mood throughout the day:

Mood Chart

12:00 AM
9:36 PM
7:12 PM
4:48 PM
2:24 PM
12:00 PM
9:36 AM
7:12 AM
4:48 AM
2:24 AM
12:00 AM

Happy   Motivated   Anxious   Manic   Stable   Sad   Frustrated   Angry   Depressed   Tired

Becka's Best Publishing

# Self- Reflection:

Things you did today to achieve your goals: _____

_____

_____

_____

Things you did today that hindered your goals: _____

_____

_____

_____

Things that went well: _____

_____

_____

_____

Things that could have gone better: _____

_____

_____

_____

Notes: _____

_____

_____

_____

Becka's Best Publishing

Date: _____ Day: _____ Time: _____

Daily Goal: _____

## To-Do List

- ○
- ○
- ○
- ○

## Daily Habits

- ○ Drink Water
- ○ Personal Hygiene
- ○ Exercise
- ○ Meditate
- ○ Eat a healthy meal

# Sleep:

Quality: _____        Wake-Up: _____

Hours: _____        Bedtime: _____

# Chart your mood throughout the day:

Mood Chart

| | |
|---|---|
| 12:00 AM | |
| 9:36 PM | |
| 7:12 PM | |
| 4:48 PM | |
| 2:24 PM | |
| 12:00 PM | |
| 9:36 AM | |
| 7:12 AM | |
| 4:48 AM | |
| 2:24 AM | |
| 12:00 AM | |

Happy   Motivated   Anxious   Manic   Stable   Sad   Frustrated   Angry   Depressed   Tired

Becka's Best Publishing

# Self- Reflection:

Things you did today to achieve your goals: _____

_____

_____

_____

Things you did today that hindered your goals: _____

_____

_____

_____

Things that went well: _____

_____

_____

_____

Things that could have gone better: _____

_____

_____

_____

Notes: _____

_____

_____

_____

Becka's Best Publishing

Date: _____ Day: _____ Time: _____

Daily Goal: _____

## To- Do List

- ○
- ○
- ○
- ○

## Daily Habits

- ○ Drink Water
- ○ Personal Hygiene
- ○ Exercise
- ○ Meditate
- ○ Eat a healthy meal

# Sleep:

Quality: _____          Wake-Up: _____

Hours: _____          Bedtime: _____

# Chart your mood throughout the day:

Mood Chart

| | Happy | Motivated | Anxious | Manic | Stable | Sad | Frustrated | Angry | Depressed | Tired |
|---|---|---|---|---|---|---|---|---|---|---|
| 12:00 AM | | | | | | | | | | |
| 9:36 PM | | | | | | | | | | |
| 7:12 PM | | | | | | | | | | |
| 4:48 PM | | | | | | | | | | |
| 2:24 PM | | | | | | | | | | |
| 12:00 PM | | | | | | | | | | |
| 9:36 AM | | | | | | | | | | |
| 7:12 AM | | | | | | | | | | |
| 4:48 AM | | | | | | | | | | |
| 2:24 AM | | | | | | | | | | |
| 12:00 AM | | | | | | | | | | |

Becka's Best Publishing

# Self- Reflection:

Things you did today to achieve your goals: _____

_____

_____

_____

Things you did today that hindered your goals: _____

_____

_____

_____

Things that went well: _____

_____

_____

_____

Things that could have gone better: _____

_____

_____

_____

Notes: _____

_____

_____

_____

Becka's Best Publishing

Date: _____ Day: _____ Time: _____

Daily Goal: _____

## To- Do List

○

○

○

○

## Daily Habits

○ Drink Water

○ Personal Hygiene

○ Exercise

○ Meditate

○ Eat a healthy meal

# Sleep:

Quality: _____        Wake-Up: _____

Hours: _____        Bedtime: _____

# Chart your mood throughout the day:

Mood Chart

| 12:00 AM |
| 9:36 PM |
| 7:12 PM |
| 4:48 PM |
| 2:24 PM |
| 12:00 PM |
| 9:36 AM |
| 7:12 AM |
| 4:48 AM |
| 2:24 AM |
| 12:00 AM |

Happy  Motivated  Anxious  Manic  Stable  Sad  Frustrated  Angry  Depressed  Tired

Becka's Best Publishing

# Self- Reflection:

Things you did today to achieve your goals: _____

_____

_____

_____

Things you did today that hindered your goals: _____

_____

_____

_____

Things that went well: _____

_____

_____

_____

Things that could have gone better: _____

_____

_____

_____

Notes: _____

_____

_____

_____

Becka's Best Publishing

Date: _____ Day: _____ Time: _____

Daily Goal: _____

## To- Do List

- ○
- ○
- ○
- ○

## Daily Habits

- ○ Drink Water
- ○ Personal Hygiene
- ○ Exercise
- ○ Meditate
- ○ Eat a healthy meal

## Sleep:

Quality: _____      Wake-Up; _____

Hours: _____      Bedtime: _____

# Chart your mood throughout the day:

Mood Chart

| | Happy | Motivated | Anxious | Manic | Stable | Sad | Frustrated | Angry | Depressed | Tired |
|---|---|---|---|---|---|---|---|---|---|---|
| 12:00 AM | | | | | | | | | | |
| 9:36 PM | | | | | | | | | | |
| 7:12 PM | | | | | | | | | | |
| 4:48 PM | | | | | | | | | | |
| 2:24 PM | | | | | | | | | | |
| 12:00 PM | | | | | | | | | | |
| 9:36 AM | | | | | | | | | | |
| 7:12 AM | | | | | | | | | | |
| 4:48 AM | | | | | | | | | | |
| 2:24 AM | | | | | | | | | | |
| 12:00 AM | | | | | | | | | | |

Becka's Best Publishing

# Self- Reflection:

Things you did today to achieve your goals: _____

_____

_____

_____

Things you did today that hindered your goals: _____

_____

_____

_____

Things that went well: _____

_____

_____

_____

Things that could have gone better: _____

_____

_____

_____

Notes: _____

_____

_____

_____

Becka's Best Publishing

Date: _____ Day: _____ Time: _____

Daily Goal: _____

To- Do List

○

○

○

○

## Daily Habits

- ○ Drink Water
- ○ Personal Hygiene
- ○ Exercise
- ○ Meditate
- ○ Eat a healthy meal

# Sleep:

Quality: _____          Wake-Up: _____

Hours: _____          Bedtime: _____

# Chart your mood throughout the day:

Mood Chart

| 12:00 AM |
| 9:36 PM |
| 7:12 PM |
| 4:48 PM |
| 2:24 PM |
| 12:00 PM |
| 9:36 AM |
| 7:12 AM |
| 4:48 AM |
| 2:24 AM |
| 12:00 AM |

Happy    Motivated    Anxious    Manic    Stable    Sad    Frustrated    Angry    Depressed    Tired

Becka's Best Publishing

# Self- Reflection:

Things you did today to achieve your goals: _____

_____

_____

_____

Things you did today that hindered your goals: _____

_____

_____

_____

Things that went well: _____

_____

_____

_____

Things that could have gone better: _____

_____

_____

_____

Notes: _____

_____

_____

_____

Becka's Best Publishing

Date: _____ Day: _____ Time: _____

# Daily Goal: _____

## To- Do List

- ○
- ○
- ○
- ○

## Daily Habits

- ○ Drink Water
- ○ Personal Hygiene
- ○ Exercise
- ○ Meditate
- ○ Eat a healthy meal

# Sleep:

Quality: _____          Wake-Up: _____

Hours: _____               Bedtime: _____

# Chart your mood throughout the day:

Mood Chart

| | | |
|---|---|---|
| 12:00 AM | | |
| 9:36 PM | | |
| 7:12 PM | | |
| 4:48 PM | | |
| 2:24 PM | | |
| 12:00 PM | | |
| 9:36 AM | | |
| 7:12 AM | | |
| 4:48 AM | | |
| 2:24 AM | | |
| 12:00 AM | | |

Happy  Motivated  Anxious  Manic  Stable  Sad  Frustrated  Angry  Depressed  Tired

Becka's Best Publishing

# Self- Reflection:

Things you did today to achieve your goals: _____

_____

_____

_____

Things you did today that hindered your goals: _____

_____

_____

_____

Things that went well: _____

_____

_____

_____

Things that could have gone better: _____

_____

_____

_____

Notes: _____

_____

_____

_____

Becka's Best Publishing

Date: _____ Day: _____ Time: _____

Daily Goal: _____

To- Do List

○

○

○

○

Daily Habits

- ○ Drink Water
- ○ Personal Hygiene
- ○ Exercise
- ○ Meditate
- ○ Eat a healthy meal

# Sleep:

Quality: _____          Wake-Up: _____

Hours: ____          Bedtime: _____

# Chart your mood throughout the day:

Mood Chart

12:00 AM
9:36 PM
7:12 PM
4:48 PM
2:24 PM
12:00 PM
9:36 AM
7:12 AM
4:48 AM
2:24 AM
12:00 AM

Happy   Motivated   Anxious   Manic   Stable   Sad   Frustrated   Angry   Depressed   Tired

# Self- Reflection:

Things you did today to achieve your goals: _____
_____
_____
_____

Things you did today that hindered your goals: _____
_____
_____
_____

Things that went well: _____
_____
_____
_____

Things that could have gone better: _____
_____
_____
_____

Notes: _____
_____
_____
_____

Becka's Best Publishing

Date: _____ Day: _____ Time: _____

Daily Goal: _____

## To- Do List

○

○

○

○

## Daily Habits

○ Drink Water

○ Personal Hygiene

○ Exercise

○ Meditate

○ Eat a healthy meal

# Sleep:

Quality: _____        Wake-Up: _____

Hours: _____        Bedtime: _____

# Chart your mood throughout the day:

Mood Chart

| | |
|---|---|
| 12:00 AM | |
| 9:36 PM | |
| 7:12 PM | |
| 4:48 PM | |
| 2:24 PM | |
| 12:00 PM | |
| 9:36 AM | |
| 7:12 AM | |
| 4:48 AM | |
| 2:24 AM | |
| 12:00 AM | |

Happy   Motivated   Anxious   Manic   Stable   Sad   Frustrated   Angry   Depressed   Tired

Becka's Best Publishing

# Self- Reflection:

Things you did today to achieve your goals: _____
_____
_____
_____

Things you did today that hindered your goals: _____
_____
_____
_____

Things that went well: _____
_____
_____
_____

Things that could have gone better: _____
_____
_____
_____

Notes: _____
_____
_____
_____

Becka's Best Publishing

Date: _____ Day: _____ Time: _____

Daily Goal: _____

## To- Do List

- ○
- ○
- ○
- ○

## Daily Habits

- ○ Drink Water
- ○ Personal Hygiene
- ○ Exercise
- ○ Meditate
- ○ Eat a healthy meal

# Sleep:

Quality: _____          Wake-Up: _____

Hours: _____          Bedtime: _____

# Chart your mood throughout the day:

Mood Chart

| 12:00 AM |
| 9:36 PM |
| 7:12 PM |
| 4:48 PM |
| 2:24 PM |
| 12:00 PM |
| 9:36 AM |
| 7:12 AM |
| 4:48 AM |
| 2:24 AM |
| 12:00 AM |

Happy  Motivated  Anxious  Manic  Stable  Sad  Frustrated  Angry  Depressed  Tired

Becka's Best Publishing

# Self- Reflection:

Things you did today to achieve your goals: _____

_____

_____

_____

Things you did today that hindered your goals: _____

_____

_____

_____

Things that went well: _____

_____

_____

_____

Things that could have gone better: _____

_____

_____

_____

Notes: _____

_____

_____

_____

Becka's Best Publishing

Date: _____ Day: _____ Time: _____

Daily Goal: _____

## To- Do List

- ○
- ○
- ○
- ○

## Daily Habits

- ○ Drink Water
- ○ Personal Hygiene
- ○ Exercise
- ○ Meditate
- ○ Eat a healthy meal

## Sleep:

Quality: _____          Wake-Up: _____

Hours: _____          Bedtime: _____

## Chart your mood throughout the day:

Mood Chart

| | |
|---|---|
| 12:00 AM | |
| 9:36 PM | |
| 7:12 PM | |
| 4:48 PM | |
| 2:24 PM | |
| 12:00 PM | |
| 9:36 AM | |
| 7:12 AM | |
| 4:48 AM | |
| 2:24 AM | |
| 12:00 AM | |

Happy  Motivated  Anxious  Manic  Stable  Sad  Frustrated  Angry  Depressed  Tired

Becka's Best Publishing

# Self- Reflection:

Things you did today to achieve your goals: _____

_____

_____

_____

Things you did today that hindered your goals: _____

_____

_____

_____

Things that went well: _____

_____

_____

_____

Things that could have gone better: _____

_____

_____

_____

Notes: _____

_____

_____

_____

Becka's Best Publishing

Date: _____ Day: _____ Time: _____

Daily Goal: _____

## To-Do List

- ○
- ○
- ○
- ○

## Daily Habits

- ○ Drink Water
- ○ Personal Hygiene
- ○ Exercise
- ○ Meditate
- ○ Eat a healthy meal

## Sleep:

Quality: _____        Wake-Up: _____

Hours: _____        Bedtime: _____

## Chart your mood throughout the day:

Mood Chart

| | Happy | Motivated | Anxious | Manic | Stable | Sad | Frustrated | Angry | Depressed | Tired |
|---|---|---|---|---|---|---|---|---|---|---|
| 12:00 AM | | | | | | | | | | |
| 9:36 PM | | | | | | | | | | |
| 7:12 PM | | | | | | | | | | |
| 4:48 PM | | | | | | | | | | |
| 2:24 PM | | | | | | | | | | |
| 12:00 PM | | | | | | | | | | |
| 9:36 AM | | | | | | | | | | |
| 7:12 AM | | | | | | | | | | |
| 4:48 AM | | | | | | | | | | |
| 2:24 AM | | | | | | | | | | |
| 12:00 AM | | | | | | | | | | |

Becka's Best Publishing

# Self- Reflection:

Things you did today to achieve your goals: _____

_____

_____

_____

Things you did today that hindered your goals: _____

_____

_____

_____

Things that went well: _____

_____

_____

_____

Things that could have gone better: _____

_____

_____

_____

Notes: _____

_____

_____

_____

Becka's Best Publishing

Date: _____ Day: _____ Time: _____

## Daily Goal: _____

## To- Do List

- ○
- ○
- ○
- ○

## Daily Habits

- ○ Drink Water
- ○ Personal Hygiene
- ○ Exercise
- ○ Meditate
- ○ Eat a healthy meal

# Sleep:

Quality: _____        Wake-Up: _____

Hours: _____        Bedtime: _____

# Chart your mood throughout the day:

Mood Chart

| | Happy | Motivated | Anxious | Manic | Stable | Sad | Frustrated | Angry | Depressed | Tired |
|---|---|---|---|---|---|---|---|---|---|---|
| 12:00 AM | | | | | | | | | | |
| 9:36 PM | | | | | | | | | | |
| 7:12 PM | | | | | | | | | | |
| 4:48 PM | | | | | | | | | | |
| 2:24 PM | | | | | | | | | | |
| 12:00 PM | | | | | | | | | | |
| 9:36 AM | | | | | | | | | | |
| 7:12 AM | | | | | | | | | | |
| 4:48 AM | | | | | | | | | | |
| 2:24 AM | | | | | | | | | | |
| 12:00 AM | | | | | | | | | | |

Becka's Best Publishing

# Self- Reflection:

Things you did today to achieve your goals: _____

_____

_____

_____

Things you did today that hindered your goals: _____

_____

_____

_____

Things that went well: _____

_____

_____

_____

Things that could have gone better: _____

_____

_____

_____

Notes: _____

_____

_____

_____

Becka's Best Publishing

Date: _____ Day: _____ Time: _____

Daily Goal: _____

## To- Do List

- ○
- ○
- ○
- ○

## Daily Habits

- ○ Drink Water
- ○ Personal Hygiene
- ○ Exercise
- ○ Meditate
- ○ Eat a healthy meal

# Sleep:

Quality: _____     Wake-Up: _____

Hours: ____     Bedtime: _____

# Chart your mood throughout the day:

Mood Chart

|  | |
|------|---|
| 12:00 AM | |
| 9:36 PM | |
| 7:12 PM | |
| 4:48 PM | |
| 2:24 PM | |
| 12:00 PM | |
| 9:36 AM | |
| 7:12 AM | |
| 4:48 AM | |
| 2:24 AM | |
| 12:00 AM | |

Happy   Motivated   Anxious   Manic   Stable   Sad   Frustrated   Angry   Depressed   Tired

Becka's Best Publishing

# Self- Reflection:

Things you did today to achieve your goals: _____

_____

_____

_____

Things you did today that hindered your goals: _____

_____

_____

_____

Things that went well: _____

_____

_____

_____

Things that could have gone better: _____

_____

_____

_____

Notes: _____

_____

_____

_____

Becka's Best Publishing

Date: _____ Day: _____ Time: _____

Daily Goal: _____

## To- Do List

○

○

○

○

○

## Daily Habits

- ○ Drink Water
- ○ Personal Hygiene
- ○ Exercise
- ○ Meditate
- ○ Eat a healthy meal

# Sleep:

Quality: _____          Wake-Up: _____

Hours: _____          Bedtime: _____

# Chart your mood throughout the day:

Mood Chart

| | Happy | Motivated | Anxious | Manic | Stable | Sad | Frustrated | Angry | Depressed | Tired |
|---|---|---|---|---|---|---|---|---|---|---|
| 12:00 AM | | | | | | | | | | |
| 9:36 PM | | | | | | | | | | |
| 7:12 PM | | | | | | | | | | |
| 4:48 PM | | | | | | | | | | |
| 2:24 PM | | | | | | | | | | |
| 12:00 PM | | | | | | | | | | |
| 9:36 AM | | | | | | | | | | |
| 7:12 AM | | | | | | | | | | |
| 4:48 AM | | | | | | | | | | |
| 2:24 AM | | | | | | | | | | |
| 12:00 AM | | | | | | | | | | |

Becka's Best Publishing

# Self- Reflection:

Things you did today to achieve your goals: _____

_____

_____

_____

Things you did today that hindered your goals: _____

_____

_____

_____

Things that went well: _____

_____

_____

_____

Things that could have gone better: _____

_____

_____

_____

Notes: _____

_____

_____

_____

Becka's Best Publishing

Date: _____ Day: _____ Time: _____

Daily Goal: _____

## To- Do List

- ○
- ○
- ○
- ○

## Daily Habits

- ○ Drink Water
- ○ Personal Hygiene
- ○ Exercise
- ○ Meditate
- ○ Eat a healthy meal

# Sleep:

Quality: _____ Wake-Up: _____

Hours: ____ Bedtime: _____

# Chart your mood throughout the day:

Mood Chart

12:00 AM
9:36 PM
7:12 PM
4:48 PM
2:24 PM
12:00 PM
9:36 AM
7:12 AM
4:48 AM
2:24 AM
12:00 AM

Happy  Motivated  Anxious  Manic  Stable  Sad  Frustrated  Angry  Depressed  Tired

# Self- Reflection:

Things you did today to achieve your goals: _____

_____

_____

_____

Things you did today that hindered your goals: _____

_____

_____

_____

Things that went well: _____

_____

_____

_____

Things that could have gone better: _____

_____

_____

_____

Notes: _____

_____

_____

_____

Becka's Best Publishing

Date: _____ Day: _____ Time: _____

Daily Goal: _____

## To-Do List

- ○
- ○
- ○
- ○

## Daily Habits

- ○ Drink Water
- ○ Personal Hygiene
- ○ Exercise
- ○ Meditate
- ○ Eat a healthy meal

# Sleep:

Quality: _____     Wake-Up: _____

Hours: _____     Bedtime: _____

# Chart your mood throughout the day:

Mood Chart

| 12:00 AM |
| 9:36 PM |
| 7:12 PM |
| 4:48 PM |
| 2:24 PM |
| 12:00 PM |
| 9:36 AM |
| 7:12 AM |
| 4:48 AM |
| 2:24 AM |
| 12:00 AM |

Happy  Motivated  Anxious  Manic  Stable  Sad  Frustrated  Angry  Depressed  Tire

Becka's Best Publishing

# Self- Reflection:

Things you did today to achieve your goals: _____
_____
_____
_____

Things you did today that hindered your goals: _____
_____
_____
_____

Things that went well: _____
_____
_____
_____

Things that could have gone better: _____
_____
_____
_____

Notes: _____
_____
_____
_____

Becka's Best Publishing

Date: _____ Day: _____ Time: _____

Daily Goal: _____

## To- Do List

- ○
- ○
- ○
- ○

## Daily Habits

- ○ Drink Water
- ○ Personal Hygiene
- ○ Exercise
- ○ Meditate
- ○ Eat a healthy meal

## Sleep:

Quality: _____          Wake-Up; _____

Hours: _____          Bedtime: _____

## Chart your mood throughout the day:

Mood Chart

|  | |
|------|---|
| 12:00 AM | |
| 9:36 PM | |
| 7:12 PM | |
| 4:48 PM | |
| 2:24 PM | |
| 12:00 PM | |
| 9:36 AM | |
| 7:12 AM | |
| 4:48 AM | |
| 2:24 AM | |
| 12:00 AM | |

Happy  Motivated  Anxious  Manic  Stable  Sad  Frustrated  Angry  Depressed  Tired

Becka's Best Publishing

# Self- Reflection:

Things you did today to achieve your goals: _____

_____

_____

_____

Things you did today that hindered your goals: _____

_____

_____

_____

Things that went well: _____

_____

_____

_____

Things that could have gone better: _____

_____

_____

_____

Notes: _____

_____

_____

_____

Becka's Best Publishing

Date: _____ Day: _____ Time: _____

Daily Goal: _____

## To- Do List

- ○
- ○
- ○
- ○

## Daily Habits

- ○ Drink Water
- ○ Personal Hygiene
- ○ Exercise
- ○ Meditate
- ○ Eat a healthy meal

# Sleep:

Quality: _____     Wake-Up: _____

Hours: _____     Bedtime: _____

# Chart your mood throughout the day:

Mood Chart

| | |
|---|---|
| 12:00 AM | |
| 9:36 PM | |
| 7:12 PM | |
| 4:48 PM | |
| 2:24 PM | |
| 12:00 PM | |
| 9:36 AM | |
| 7:12 AM | |
| 4:48 AM | |
| 2:24 AM | |
| 12:00 AM | |

Happy   Motivated   Anxious   Manic   Stable   Sad   Frustrated   Angry   Depressed   Tired

Becka's Best Publishing

# Self- Reflection:

Things you did today to achieve your goals: _____

_____

_____

_____

Things you did today that hindered your goals: _____

_____

_____

_____

Things that went well: _____

_____

_____

_____

Things that could have gone better: _____

_____

_____

_____

Notes: _____

_____

_____

_____

Becka's Best Publishing

Date: _____ Day: _____ Time: _____

Daily Goal: _____

## To-Do List

- ○
- ○
- ○
- ○

## Daily Habits

- ○ Drink Water
- ○ Personal Hygiene
- ○ Exercise
- ○ Meditate
- ○ Eat a healthy meal

## Sleep:

Quality: _____          Wake-Up: _____

Hours: _____          Bedtime: _____

## Chart your mood throughout the day:

Mood Chart

| 12:00 AM |
| 9:36 PM |
| 7:12 PM |
| 4:48 PM |
| 2:24 PM |
| 12:00 PM |
| 9:36 AM |
| 7:12 AM |
| 4:48 AM |
| 2:24 AM |
| 12:00 AM |

Happy   Motivated   Anxious   Manic   Stable   Sad   Frustrated   Angry   Depressed   Tired

Becka's Best Publishing

# Self- Reflection:

Things you did today to achieve your goals: _____

_____

_____

_____

Things you did today that hindered your goals: _____

_____

_____

_____

Things that went well: _____

_____

_____

_____

Things that could have gone better: _____

_____

_____

_____

Notes: _____

_____

_____

_____

Becka's Best Publishing

Date: _____ Day: _____ Time: _____

Daily Goal: _____

## To- Do List

○

○

○

○

## Daily Habits

○ Drink Water

○ Personal Hygiene

○ Exercise

○ Meditate

○ Eat a healthy meal

# Sleep:

Quality: _____          Wake-Up: _____

Hours: ____          Bedtime: _____

# Chart your mood throughout the day:

Mood Chart

|  |
|------|
| 12:00 AM |
| 9:36 PM |
| 7:12 PM |
| 4:48 PM |
| 2:24 PM |
| 12:00 PM |
| 9:36 AM |
| 7:12 AM |
| 4:48 AM |
| 2:24 AM |
| 12:00 AM |

Happy   Motivated   Anxious   Manic   Stable   Sad   Frustrated   Angry   Depressed   Tired

Becka's Best Publishing

# Self- Reflection:

Things you did today to achieve your goals: _____

_____

_____

_____

Things you did today that hindered your goals: _____

_____

_____

_____

Things that went well: _____

_____

_____

_____

Things that could have gone better: _____

_____

_____

_____

Notes: _____

_____

_____

_____

Becka's Best Publishing

Date: _____ Day: _____ Time: _____

Daily Goal: _____

## To- Do List

○

○

○

○

## Daily Habits

○ Drink Water

○ Personal Hygiene

○ Exercise

○ Meditate

○ Eat a healthy meal

# Sleep:

Quality: _____          Wake-Up: _____

Hours: _____          Bedtime: _____

# Chart your mood throughout the day:

Mood Chart

|  | |
|------|--|
| 12:00 AM | |
| 9:36 PM | |
| 7:12 PM | |
| 4:48 PM | |
| 2:24 PM | |
| 12:00 PM | |
| 9:36 AM | |
| 7:12 AM | |
| 4:48 AM | |
| 2:24 AM | |
| 12:00 AM | |

Happy  Motivated  Anxious  Manic  Stable  Sad  Frustrated  Angry  Depressed  Tired

Becka's Best Publishing

# Self- Reflection:

Things you did today to achieve your goals: _____

_____

_____

_____

Things you did today that hindered your goals: _____

_____

_____

_____

Things that went well: _____

_____

_____

_____

Things that could have gone better: _____

_____

_____

_____

Notes: _____

_____

_____

_____

Becka's Best Publishing

Date: _____ Day: _____ Time: _____

Daily Goal: _____

## To- Do List

- ○
- ○
- ○
- ○

## Daily Habits

- ○  Drink Water
- ○  Personal Hygiene
- ○  Exercise
- ○  Meditate
- ○  Eat a healthy meal

## Sleep:

Quality: _____          Wake-Up; _____

Hours: ____          Bedtime: _____

## Chart your mood throughout the day:

Mood Chart

12:00 AM
9:36 PM
7:12 PM
4:48 PM
2:24 PM
12:00 PM
9:36 AM
7:12 AM
4:48 AM
2:24 AM
12:00 AM

Happy  Motivated  Anxious  Manic  Stable  Sad  Frustrated  Angry  Depressed  Tired

Becka's Best Publishing

# Self-Reflection:

Things you did today to achieve your goals: _____
_____
_____
_____

Things you did today that hindered your goals: _____
_____
_____
_____

Things that went well: _____
_____
_____
_____

Things that could have gone better: _____
_____
_____
_____

Notes: _____
_____
_____
_____

Becka's Best Publishing

Date: _____ Day: _____ Time: _____

Daily Goal: _____

## To- Do List

○

○

○

○

## Daily Habits

- ○ Drink Water
- ○ Personal Hygiene
- ○ Exercise
- ○ Meditate
- ○ Eat a healthy meal

## Sleep:

Quality: _____    Wake-Up: _____

Hours: _____    Bedtime: _____

## Chart your mood throughout the day:

### Mood Chart

12:00 AM
9:36 PM
7:12 PM
4:48 PM
2:24 PM
12:00 PM
9:36 AM
7:12 AM
4:48 AM
2:24 AM
12:00 AM

Happy  Motivated  Anxious  Manic  Stable  Sad  Frustrated  Angry  Depressed  Tired

Becka's Best Publishing

# Self- Reflection:

Things you did today to achieve your goals: _____

_____

_____

_____

Things you did today that hindered your goals: _____

_____

_____

_____

Things that went well: _____

_____

_____

_____

Things that could have gone better: _____

_____

_____

_____

Notes: _____

_____

_____

_____

Becka's Best Publishing

Date: _____ Day: _____ Time: _____

## Daily Goal: _____

To- Do List

○

○

○

○

Daily Habits

- ○ Drink Water
- ○ Personal Hygiene
- ○ Exercise
- ○ Meditate
- ○ Eat a healthy meal

## Sleep:

Quality: _____          Wake-Up: _____

Hours: ____          Bedtime: _____

## Chart your mood throughout the day:

Mood Chart

|  |
|------|
| 12:00 AM |
| 9:36 PM |
| 7:12 PM |
| 4:48 PM |
| 2:24 PM |
| 12:00 PM |
| 9:36 AM |
| 7:12 AM |
| 4:48 AM |
| 2:24 AM |
| 12:00 AM |

Happy  Motivated  Anxious  Manic  Stable  Sad  Frustrated  Angry  Depressed  Tired

Becka's Best Publishing

# Self- Reflection:

Things you did today to achieve your goals: _____

_____

_____

_____

Things you did today that hindered your goals: _____

_____

_____

_____

Things that went well: _____

_____

_____

_____

Things that could have gone better: _____

_____

_____

_____

Notes: _____

_____

_____

_____

Becka's Best Publishing

Date: _____ Day: _____ Time: _____

Daily Goal: _____

## To- Do List

- ○
- ○
- ○
- ○

## Daily Habits

- ○ Drink Water
- ○ Personal Hygiene
- ○ Exercise
- ○ Meditate
- ○ Eat a healthy meal

## Sleep:

Quality: _____        Wake-Up: _____

Hours: ____        Bedtime: _____

## Chart your mood throughout the day:

Mood Chart

|  |
|------|
| 12:00 AM |
| 9:36 PM |
| 7:12 PM |
| 4:48 PM |
| 2:24 PM |
| 12:00 PM |
| 9:36 AM |
| 7:12 AM |
| 4:48 AM |
| 2:24 AM |
| 12:00 AM |

Happy  Motivated  Anxious  Manic  Stable  Sad  Frustrated  Angry  Depressed  Tired

Becka's Best Publishing

# Self- Reflection:

Things you did today to achieve your goals: _____

_____

_____

_____

Things you did today that hindered your goals: _____

_____

_____

_____

Things that went well: _____

_____

_____

_____

Things that could have gone better: _____

_____

_____

_____

Notes: _____

_____

_____

_____

Becka's Best Publishing

Date: _____ Day: _____ Time: _____

## Daily Goal: _____

To- Do List

○

○

○

○

Daily Habits

    ○   Drink Water

    ○   Personal Hygiene

    ○   Exercise

    ○   Meditate

    ○   Eat a healthy meal

## Sleep:

Quality: _____          Wake-Up; _____

Hours: ____          Bedtime: _____

## Chart your mood throughout the day:

Mood Chart

| | 12:00 AM |
| 9:36 PM |
| 7:12 PM |
| 4:48 PM |
| 2:24 PM |
| 12:00 PM |
| 9:36 AM |
| 7:12 AM |
| 4:48 AM |
| 2:24 AM |
| 12:00 AM |

Happy   Motivated   Anxious   Manic   Stable   Sad   Frustrated   Angry   Depressed   Tired

Becka's Best Publishing

# Self- Reflection:

Things you did today to achieve your goals: _____
_____
_____
_____

Things you did today that hindered your goals: _____
_____
_____
_____

Things that went well: _____
_____
_____
_____

Things that could have gone better: _____
_____
_____
_____

Notes: _____
_____
_____
_____

Becka's Best Publishing

Date: _____ Day: _____ Time: _____

Daily Goal: _____

## To- Do List

- ○
- ○
- ○
- ○

## Daily Habits

- ○ Drink Water
- ○ Personal Hygiene
- ○ Exercise
- ○ Meditate
- ○ Eat a healthy meal

# Sleep:

Quality: _____   Wake-Up: _____

Hours: _____   Bedtime: _____

# Chart your mood throughout the day:

Mood Chart

|  |
| --- |
| 12:00 AM |
| 9:36 PM |
| 7:12 PM |
| 4:48 PM |
| 2:24 PM |
| 12:00 PM |
| 9:36 AM |
| 7:12 AM |
| 4:48 AM |
| 2:24 AM |
| 12:00 AM |

Happy  Motivated  Anxious  Manic  Stable  Sad  Frustrated  Angry  Depressed  Tired

Becka's Best Publishing

# Self- Reflection:

Things you did today to achieve your goals: _____

_____

_____

_____

Things you did today that hindered your goals: _____

_____

_____

_____

Things that went well: _____

_____

_____

_____

Things that could have gone better: _____

_____

_____

_____

Notes: _____

_____

_____

_____

Becka's Best Publishing

Date: _____ Day: _____ Time: _____

Daily Goal: _____

## To- Do List

○

○

○

○

## Daily Habits

- ○ Drink Water
- ○ Personal Hygiene
- ○ Exercise
- ○ Meditate
- ○ Eat a healthy meal

# Sleep:

Quality: _____        Wake-Up: _____

Hours: ____        Bedtime: _____

# Chart your mood throughout the day:

Mood Chart

12:00 AM
9:36 PM
7:12 PM
4:48 PM
2:24 PM
12:00 PM
9:36 AM
7:12 AM
4:48 AM
2:24 AM
12:00 AM

Happy   Motivated   Anxious   Manic   Stable   Sad   Frustrated   Angry   Depressed   Tired

# Self- Reflection:

Things you did today to achieve your goals: _____

_____

_____

_____

Things you did today that hindered your goals: _____

_____

_____

_____

Things that went well: _____

_____

_____

_____

Things that could have gone better: _____

_____

_____

_____

Notes: _____

_____

_____

_____

Becka's Best Publishing

Date: _____ Day: _____ Time: _____

Daily Goal: _____

## To- Do List

- ○
- ○
- ○
- ○

## Daily Habits

- ○ Drink Water
- ○ Personal Hygiene
- ○ Exercise
- ○ Meditate
- ○ Eat a healthy meal

# Sleep:

Quality: _____        Wake-Up: _____

Hours: _____        Bedtime: _____

# Chart your mood throughout the day:

Mood Chart

| Time | Happy | Motivated | Anxious | Manic | Stable | Sad | Frustrated | Angry | Depressed | Tired |
|------|-------|-----------|---------|-------|--------|-----|------------|-------|-----------|-------|
| 12:00 AM | | | | | | | | | | |
| 9:36 PM | | | | | | | | | | |
| 7:12 PM | | | | | | | | | | |
| 4:48 PM | | | | | | | | | | |
| 2:24 PM | | | | | | | | | | |
| 12:00 PM | | | | | | | | | | |
| 9:36 AM | | | | | | | | | | |
| 7:12 AM | | | | | | | | | | |
| 4:48 AM | | | | | | | | | | |
| 2:24 AM | | | | | | | | | | |
| 12:00 AM | | | | | | | | | | |

Becka's Best Publishing

# Self- Reflection:

Things you did today to achieve your goals: _____

_____

_____

_____

Things you did today that hindered your goals: _____

_____

_____

_____

Things that went well: _____

_____

_____

_____

Things that could have gone better: _____

_____

_____

_____

Notes: _____

_____

_____

_____

Becka's Best Publishing

Date: _____ Day: _____ Time: _____

Daily Goal: _____

To- Do List

- ○
- ○
- ○
- ○
- ○

Daily Habits

- ○ Drink Water
- ○ Personal Hygiene
- ○ Exercise
- ○ Meditate
- ○ Eat a healthy meal

# Sleep:

Quality: _____  Wake-Up: _____

Hours: _____  Bedtime: _____

# Chart your mood throughout the day:

Mood Chart

| | Happy | Motivated | Anxious | Manic | Stable | Sad | Frustrated | Angry | Depressed | Tired |
|---|---|---|---|---|---|---|---|---|---|---|
| 12:00 AM | | | | | | | | | | |
| 9:36 PM | | | | | | | | | | |
| 7:12 PM | | | | | | | | | | |
| 4:48 PM | | | | | | | | | | |
| 2:24 PM | | | | | | | | | | |
| 12:00 PM | | | | | | | | | | |
| 9:36 AM | | | | | | | | | | |
| 7:12 AM | | | | | | | | | | |
| 4:48 AM | | | | | | | | | | |
| 2:24 AM | | | | | | | | | | |
| 12:00 AM | | | | | | | | | | |

Becka's Best Publishing

# Self- Reflection:

Things you did today to achieve your goals: _____

_____

_____

_____

Things you did today that hindered your goals: _____

_____

_____

_____

Things that went well: _____

_____

_____

_____

Things that could have gone better: _____

_____

_____

_____

Notes: _____

_____

_____

_____

Becka's Best Publishing

Date: _____ Day: _____ Time: _____

Daily Goal: _____

## To- Do List

- ○
- ○
- ○
- ○

## Daily Habits

- ○ Drink Water
- ○ Personal Hygiene
- ○ Exercise
- ○ Meditate
- ○ Eat a healthy meal

## Sleep:

Quality: _____     Wake-Up: _____

Hours: _____     Bedtime: _____

## Chart your mood throughout the day:

Mood Chart

```
12:00 AM
 9:36 PM
 7:12 PM
 4:48 PM
 2:24 PM
12:00 PM
 9:36 AM
 7:12 AM
 4:48 AM
 2:24 AM
12:00 AM
         Happy  Motivated  Anxious  Manic  Stable  Sad  Frustrated  Angry  Depressed  Tired
```

Becka's Best Publishing

# Self- Reflection:

Things you did today to achieve your goals: _____

_____

_____

_____

Things you did today that hindered your goals: _____

_____

_____

_____

Things that went well: _____

_____

_____

_____

Things that could have gone better: _____

_____

_____

_____

Notes: _____

_____

_____

_____

Becka's Best Publishing

Date: _____ Day: _____ Time: _____

Daily Goal: _____

## To- Do List

- ○
- ○
- ○
- ○

## Daily Habits

- ○ Drink Water
- ○ Personal Hygiene
- ○ Exercise
- ○ Meditate
- ○ Eat a healthy meal

## Sleep:

Quality: _____          Wake-Up: _____

Hours: _____          Bedtime: _____

## Chart your mood throughout the day:

Mood Chart

12:00 AM
9:36 PM
7:12 PM
4:48 PM
2:24 PM
12:00 PM
9:36 AM
7:12 AM
4:48 AM
2:24 AM
12:00 AM

Happy  Motivated  Anxious  Manic  Stable  Sad  Frustrated  Angry  Depressed  Tired

Becka's Best Publishing

# Self- Reflection:

Things you did today to achieve your goals: _____

_____

_____

_____

Things you did today that hindered your goals: _____

_____

_____

_____

Things that went well: _____

_____

_____

_____

Things that could have gone better: _____

_____

_____

_____

Notes: _____

_____

_____

_____

Becka's Best Publishing

Date: _____ Day: _____ Time: _____

Daily Goal: _____

## To- Do List

- ○
- ○
- ○
- ○

## Daily Habits

- ○ Drink Water
- ○ Personal Hygiene
- ○ Exercise
- ○ Meditate
- ○ Eat a healthy meal

# Sleep:

Quality: _____          Wake-Up: _____

Hours: _____          Bedtime: _____

# Chart your mood throughout the day:

Mood Chart

| | Happy | Motivated | Anxious | Manic | Stable | Sad | Frustrated | Angry | Depressed | Tired |
|---|---|---|---|---|---|---|---|---|---|---|
| 12:00 AM | | | | | | | | | | |
| 9:36 PM | | | | | | | | | | |
| 7:12 PM | | | | | | | | | | |
| 4:48 PM | | | | | | | | | | |
| 2:24 PM | | | | | | | | | | |
| 12:00 PM | | | | | | | | | | |
| 9:36 AM | | | | | | | | | | |
| 7:12 AM | | | | | | | | | | |
| 4:48 AM | | | | | | | | | | |
| 2:24 AM | | | | | | | | | | |
| 12:00 AM | | | | | | | | | | |

Becka's Best Publishing

# Self- Reflection:

Things you did today to achieve your goals: _____

_____

_____

_____

Things you did today that hindered your goals: _____

_____

_____

_____

Things that went well: _____

_____

_____

_____

Things that could have gone better: _____

_____

_____

_____

Notes: _____

_____

_____

_____

Becka's Best Publishing

Date: _____ Day: _____ Time: _____

Daily Goal: _____

## To- Do List

○

○

○

○

## Daily Habits

- ○ Drink Water
- ○ Personal Hygiene
- ○ Exercise
- ○ Meditate
- ○ Eat a healthy meal

## Sleep:

Quality: _____    Wake-Up: _____

Hours: _____    Bedtime: _____

## Chart your mood throughout the day:

### Mood Chart

|  | |
|---|---|
| 12:00 AM | |
| 9:36 PM | |
| 7:12 PM | |
| 4:48 PM | |
| 2:24 PM | |
| 12:00 PM | |
| 9:36 AM | |
| 7:12 AM | |
| 4:48 AM | |
| 2:24 AM | |
| 12:00 AM | |

Happy  Motivated  Anxious  Manic  Stable  Sad  Frustrated  Angry  Depressed  Tired

Becka's Best Publishing

# Self-Reflection:

Things you did today to achieve your goals: _____

_____

_____

_____

Things you did today that hindered your goals: _____

_____

_____

_____

Things that went well: _____

_____

_____

_____

Things that could have gone better: _____

_____

_____

_____

Notes: _____

_____

_____

_____

Becka's Best Publishing

Date: _____ Day: _____ Time: _____

## Daily Goal: _____

### To- Do List

- ○
- ○
- ○
- ○

### Daily Habits

- ○ Drink Water
- ○ Personal Hygiene
- ○ Exercise
- ○ Meditate
- ○ Eat a healthy meal

## Sleep:

Quality: _____    Wake-Up: _____

Hours: _____    Bedtime: _____

## Chart your mood throughout the day:

Mood Chart

| | Happy | Motivated | Anxious | Manic | Stable | Sad | Frustrated | Angry | Depressed | Tired |
|---|---|---|---|---|---|---|---|---|---|---|
| 12:00 AM | | | | | | | | | | |
| 9:36 PM | | | | | | | | | | |
| 7:12 PM | | | | | | | | | | |
| 4:48 PM | | | | | | | | | | |
| 2:24 PM | | | | | | | | | | |
| 12:00 PM | | | | | | | | | | |
| 9:36 AM | | | | | | | | | | |
| 7:12 AM | | | | | | | | | | |
| 4:48 AM | | | | | | | | | | |
| 2:24 AM | | | | | | | | | | |
| 12:00 AM | | | | | | | | | | |

Becka's Best Publishing

# Self- Reflection:

Things you did today to achieve your goals: _____

_____

_____

_____

Things you did today that hindered your goals: _____

_____

_____

_____

Things that went well: _____

_____

_____

_____

Things that could have gone better: _____

_____

_____

_____

Notes: _____

_____

_____

_____

Becka's Best Publishing

Date: _____ Day: _____ Time: _____

Daily Goal: _____

## To- Do List

○

○

○

○

## Daily Habits

- ○ Drink Water
- ○ Personal Hygiene
- ○ Exercise
- ○ Meditate
- ○ Eat a healthy meal

# Sleep:

Quality: _____          Wake-Up: _____

Hours: _____          Bedtime: _____

# Chart your mood throughout the day:

Mood Chart

12:00 AM
9:36 PM
7:12 PM
4:48 PM
2:24 PM
12:00 PM
9:36 AM
7:12 AM
4:48 AM
2:24 AM
12:00 AM

Happy   Motivated   Anxious   Manic   Stable   Sad   Frustrated   Angry   Depressed   Tired

Becka's Best Publishing

# Self- Reflection:

Things you did today to achieve your goals: _____
_____
_____
_____

Things you did today that hindered your goals: _____
_____
_____
_____

Things that went well: _____
_____
_____
_____

Things that could have gone better: _____
_____
_____
_____

Notes: _____
_____
_____
_____

Becka's Best Publishing

Date: _____ Day: _____ Time: _____

Daily Goal: _____

## To- Do List

- ○
- ○
- ○
- ○

## Daily Habits

- ○ Drink Water
- ○ Personal Hygiene
- ○ Exercise
- ○ Meditate
- ○ Eat a healthy meal

## Sleep:

Quality: _____     Wake-Up: _____

Hours: _____     Bedtime: _____

## Chart your mood throughout the day:

Mood Chart

12:00 AM
9:36 PM
7:12 PM
4:48 PM
2:24 PM
12:00 PM
9:36 AM
7:12 AM
4:48 AM
2:24 AM
12:00 AM

Happy · Motivated · Anxious · Manic · Stable · Sad · Frustrated · Angry · Depressed · Tired

Becka's Best Publishing

# Self- Reflection:

Things you did today to achieve your goals: _____

_____

_____

_____

Things you did today that hindered your goals: _____

_____

_____

_____

Things that went well: _____

_____

_____

_____

Things that could have gone better: _____

_____

_____

_____

Notes: _____

_____

_____

_____

Becka's Best Publishing

Date: _____ Day: _____ Time: _____

Daily Goal: _____

## To- Do List

- ○
- ○
- ○
- ○

## Daily Habits

- ○ Drink Water
- ○ Personal Hygiene
- ○ Exercise
- ○ Meditate
- ○ Eat a healthy meal

# Sleep:

Quality: _____          Wake-Up: _____

Hours: _____                Bedtime: _____

# Chart your mood throughout the day:

Mood Chart

| | Happy | Motivated | Anxious | Manic | Stable | Sad | Frustrated | Angry | Depressed | Tired |
|---|---|---|---|---|---|---|---|---|---|---|
| 12:00 AM | | | | | | | | | | |
| 9:36 PM | | | | | | | | | | |
| 7:12 PM | | | | | | | | | | |
| 4:48 PM | | | | | | | | | | |
| 2:24 PM | | | | | | | | | | |
| 12:00 PM | | | | | | | | | | |
| 9:36 AM | | | | | | | | | | |
| 7:12 AM | | | | | | | | | | |
| 4:48 AM | | | | | | | | | | |
| 2:24 AM | | | | | | | | | | |
| 12:00 AM | | | | | | | | | | |

Becka's Best Publishing

# Self- Reflection:

Things you did today to achieve your goals: _____
_____
_____
_____

Things you did today that hindered your goals: _____
_____
_____
_____

Things that went well: _____
_____
_____
_____

Things that could have gone better: _____
_____
_____
_____

Notes: _____
_____
_____
_____

Becka's Best Publishing

Date: _____ Day: _____ Time: _____

Daily Goal: _____

## To- Do List

- ○
- ○
- ○
- ○

## Daily Habits

- ○ Drink Water
- ○ Personal Hygiene
- ○ Exercise
- ○ Meditate
- ○ Eat a healthy meal

# Sleep:

Quality: _____     Wake-Up: _____

Hours: _____     Bedtime: _____

# Chart your mood throughout the day:

Mood Chart

| | |
|---|---|
| 12:00 AM | |
| 9:36 PM | |
| 7:12 PM | |
| 4:48 PM | |
| 2:24 PM | |
| 12:00 PM | |
| 9:36 AM | |
| 7:12 AM | |
| 4:48 AM | |
| 2:24 AM | |
| 12:00 AM | |

Happy  Motivated  Anxious  Manic  Stable  Sad  Frustrated  Angry  Depressed  Tired

Becka's Best Publishing

# Self- Reflection:

Things you did today to achieve your goals: _____

_____

_____

_____

Things you did today that hindered your goals: _____

_____

_____

_____

Things that went well: _____

_____

_____

_____

Things that could have gone better: _____

_____

_____

_____

Notes: _____

_____

_____

_____

Becka's Best Publishing

Date: _____ Day: _____ Time: _____

Daily Goal: _____

## To- Do List

- ○
- ○
- ○
- ○

## Daily Habits

- ○ Drink Water
- ○ Personal Hygiene
- ○ Exercise
- ○ Meditate
- ○ Eat a healthy meal

## Sleep:

Quality: _____          Wake-Up: _____

Hours: _____          Bedtime: _____

## Chart your mood throughout the day:

Mood Chart

12:00 AM
9:36 PM
7:12 PM
4:48 PM
2:24 PM
12:00 PM
9:36 AM
7:12 AM
4:48 AM
2:24 AM
12:00 AM

Happy  Motivated  Anxious  Manic  Stable  Sad  Frustrated  Angry  Depressed  Tire

Becka's Best Publishing

# Self- Reflection:

Things you did today to achieve your goals: _____

_____

_____

_____

Things you did today that hindered your goals: _____

_____

_____

_____

Things that went well: _____

_____

_____

_____

Things that could have gone better: _____

_____

_____

_____

Notes: _____

_____

_____

_____

Becka's Best Publishing

Date: _____ Day: _____ Time: _____

Daily Goal: _____

## To-Do List

- ○
- ○
- ○
- ○

## Daily Habits

- ○ Drink Water
- ○ Personal Hygiene
- ○ Exercise
- ○ Meditate
- ○ Eat a healthy meal

# Sleep:

Quality: _____          Wake-Up: _____

Hours: ____          Bedtime: _____

# Chart your mood throughout the day:

Mood Chart

| 12:00 AM |
| 9:36 PM |
| 7:12 PM |
| 4:48 PM |
| 2:24 PM |
| 12:00 PM |
| 9:36 AM |
| 7:12 AM |
| 4:48 AM |
| 2:24 AM |
| 12:00 AM |

Happy   Motivated   Anxious   Manic   Stable   Sad   Frustrated   Angry   Depressed   Tired

Becka's Best Publishing

# Self- Reflection:

Things you did today to achieve your goals: _____

_____

_____

_____

Things you did today that hindered your goals: _____

_____

_____

_____

Things that went well: _____

_____

_____

_____

Things that could have gone better: _____

_____

_____

_____

Notes: _____

_____

_____

_____

Becka's Best Publishing

Date: _____ Day: _____ Time: _____

Daily Goal: _____

## To- Do List

○

○

○

○

## Daily Habits

- ○ Drink Water
- ○ Personal Hygiene
- ○ Exercise
- ○ Meditate
- ○ Eat a healthy meal

# Sleep:

Quality: _____          Wake-Up; _____

Hours: ____          Bedtime: _____

# Chart your mood throughout the day:

Mood Chart

| | |
|---|---|
| 12:00 AM | |
| 9:36 PM | |
| 7:12 PM | |
| 4:48 PM | |
| 2:24 PM | |
| 12:00 PM | |
| 9:36 AM | |
| 7:12 AM | |
| 4:48 AM | |
| 2:24 AM | |
| 12:00 AM | |

Happy   Motivated   Anxious   Manic   Stable   Sad   Frustrated   Angry   Depressed   Tired

Becka's Best Publishing

# Self- Reflection:

Things you did today to achieve your goals: _____
_____
_____
_____

Things you did today that hindered your goals: _____
_____
_____
_____

Things that went well: _____
_____
_____
_____

Things that could have gone better: _____
_____
_____
_____

Notes: _____
_____
_____

_____Date:

_____ Day: _____ Time: _____

Becka's Best Publishing

# Daily Goal: _____

## To- Do List

- ○
- ○
- ○
- ○

## Daily Habits

- ○ Drink Water
- ○ Personal Hygiene
- ○ Exercise
- ○ Meditate
- ○ Eat a healthy meal

## Sleep:

Quality: _____          Wake-Up: _____

Hours: _____          Bedtime: _____

## Chart your mood throughout the day:

### Mood Chart

| Time | Happy | Motivated | Anxious | Manic | Stable | Sad | Frustrated | Angry | Depressed | Tired |
|------|-------|-----------|---------|-------|--------|-----|------------|-------|-----------|-------|
| 12:00 AM | | | | | | | | | | |
| 9:36 PM | | | | | | | | | | |
| 7:12 PM | | | | | | | | | | |
| 4:48 PM | | | | | | | | | | |
| 2:24 PM | | | | | | | | | | |
| 12:00 PM | | | | | | | | | | |
| 9:36 AM | | | | | | | | | | |
| 7:12 AM | | | | | | | | | | |
| 4:48 AM | | | | | | | | | | |
| 2:24 AM | | | | | | | | | | |
| 12:00 AM | | | | | | | | | | |

Becka's Best Publishing

# Self- Reflection:

Things you did today to achieve your goals: _____

_____

_____

_____

Things you did today that hindered your goals: _____

_____

_____

_____

Things that went well: _____

_____

_____

_____

Things that could have gone better: _____

_____

_____

_____

Notes: _____

_____

_____

_____

Becka's Best Publishing

Date: _____ Day: _____ Time: _____

Daily Goal: _____

## To- Do List

○

○

○

○

## Daily Habits

○ Drink Water

○ Personal Hygiene

○ Exercise

○ Meditate

○ Eat a healthy meal

# Sleep:

Quality: _____          Wake-Up: _____

Hours: _____             Bedtime: _____

# Chart your mood throughout the day:

Mood Chart

| | |
|---|---|
| 12:00 AM | |
| 9:36 PM | |
| 7:12 PM | |
| 4:48 PM | |
| 2:24 PM | |
| 12:00 PM | |
| 9:36 AM | |
| 7:12 AM | |
| 4:48 AM | |
| 2:24 AM | |
| 12:00 AM | |

Happy  Motivated  Anxious  Manic  Stable  Sad  Frustrated  Angry  Depressed  Tired

Becka's Best Publishing

# Self- Reflection:

Things you did today to achieve your goals: _____
_____
_____
_____

Things you did today that hindered your goals: _____
_____
_____
_____

Things that went well: _____
_____
_____
_____

Things that could have gone better: _____
_____
_____
_____

Notes: _____
_____
_____
_____

Becka's Best Publishing

Date: _____ Day: _____ Time: _____

Daily Goal: _____

## To- Do List

○

○

○

○

## Daily Habits

- ○ Drink Water
- ○ Personal Hygiene
- ○ Exercise
- ○ Meditate
- ○ Eat a healthy meal

# Sleep:

Quality: _____     Wake-Up: _____

Hours: ____     Bedtime: _____

# Chart your mood throughout the day:

Mood Chart

| Time | Happy | Motivated | Anxious | Manic | Stable | Sad | Frustrated | Angry | Depressed | Tired |
|------|-------|-----------|---------|-------|--------|-----|------------|-------|-----------|-------|
| 12:00 AM | | | | | | | | | | |
| 9:36 PM | | | | | | | | | | |
| 7:12 PM | | | | | | | | | | |
| 4:48 PM | | | | | | | | | | |
| 2:24 PM | | | | | | | | | | |
| 12:00 PM | | | | | | | | | | |
| 9:36 AM | | | | | | | | | | |
| 7:12 AM | | | | | | | | | | |
| 4:48 AM | | | | | | | | | | |
| 2:24 AM | | | | | | | | | | |
| 12:00 AM | | | | | | | | | | |

Becka's Best Publishing

# Self- Reflection:

Things you did today to achieve your goals: _____

_____

_____

_____

Things you did today that hindered your goals: _____

_____

_____

_____

Things that went well: _____

_____

_____

_____

Things that could have gone better: _____

_____

_____

_____

Notes: _____

_____

_____

_____

Becka's Best Publishing

Date: _____ Day: _____ Time: _____

Daily Goal: _____

To- Do List                    Daily Habits

○                              ○   Drink Water

○                              ○   Personal Hygiene

○                              ○   Exercise

○                              ○   Meditate

○                              ○   Eat a healthy meal

# Sleep:

Quality: _____         Wake-Up; _____

Hours: ____              Bedtime: _____

# Chart your mood throughout the day:

Mood Chart

12:00 AM
 9:36 PM
 7:12 PM
 4:48 PM
 2:24 PM
12:00 PM
 9:36 AM
 7:12 AM
 4:48 AM
 2:24 AM
12:00 AM

Happy  Motivated  Anxious  Manic  Stable  Sad  Frustrated  Angry  Depressed  Tired

Becka's Best Publishing

# Self- Reflection:

Things you did today to achieve your goals: _____

_____

_____

_____

Things you did today that hindered your goals: _____

_____

_____

_____

Things that went well: _____

_____

_____

_____

Things that could have gone better: _____

_____

_____

_____

Notes: _____

_____

_____

_____

Becka's Best Publishing

Date: _____ Day: _____ Time: _____

**Daily Goal:** _____

## To-Do List

○

○

○

○

## Daily Habits

○ Drink Water

○ Personal Hygiene

○ Exercise

○ Meditate

○ Eat a healthy meal

# Sleep:

Quality: _____          Wake-Up: _____

Hours: _____          Bedtime: _____

# Chart your mood throughout the day:

Mood Chart

| | Happy | Motivated | Anxious | Manic | Stable | Sad | Frustrated | Angry | Depressed | Tired |
|---|---|---|---|---|---|---|---|---|---|---|
| 12:00 AM | | | | | | | | | | |
| 9:36 PM | | | | | | | | | | |
| 7:12 PM | | | | | | | | | | |
| 4:48 PM | | | | | | | | | | |
| 2:24 PM | | | | | | | | | | |
| 12:00 PM | | | | | | | | | | |
| 9:36 AM | | | | | | | | | | |
| 7:12 AM | | | | | | | | | | |
| 4:48 AM | | | | | | | | | | |
| 2:24 AM | | | | | | | | | | |
| 12:00 AM | | | | | | | | | | |

# Self- Reflection:

Things you did today to achieve your goals: _____

_____

_____

_____

Things you did today that hindered your goals: _____

_____

_____

_____

Things that went well: _____

_____

_____

_____

Things that could have gone better: _____

_____

_____

_____

Notes: _____

_____

_____

_____

Becka's Best Publishing

Date: _____ Day: _____ Time: _____

Daily Goal: _____

## To- Do List

○

○

○

○

## Daily Habits

○ Drink Water

○ Personal Hygiene

○ Exercise

○ Meditate

○ Eat a healthy meal

## Sleep:

Quality: _____          Wake-Up: _____

Hours: _____          Bedtime: _____

## Chart your mood throughout the day:

Mood Chart

12:00 AM
9:36 PM
7:12 PM
4:48 PM
2:24 PM
12:00 PM
9:36 AM
7:12 AM
4:48 AM
2:24 AM
12:00 AM

Happy  Motivated  Anxious  Manic  Stable  Sad  Frustrated  Angry  Depressed  Tired

Becka's Best Publishing

# Self- Reflection:

Things you did today to achieve your goals: _____

_____

_____

_____

Things you did today that hindered your goals: _____

_____

_____

_____

Things that went well: _____

_____

_____

_____

Things that could have gone better: _____

_____

_____

_____

Notes: _____

_____

_____

_____

Becka's Best Publishing

Date: _____ Day: _____ Time: _____

Daily Goal: _____

## To- Do List

- ○
- ○
- ○
- ○

## Daily Habits

- ○  Drink Water
- ○  Personal Hygiene
- ○  Exercise
- ○  Meditate
- ○  Eat a healthy meal

## Sleep:

Quality: _____     Wake-Up: _____

Hours: _____     Bedtime: _____

## Chart your mood throughout the day:

Mood Chart

| | |
|---|---|
| 12:00 AM | |
| 9:36 PM | |
| 7:12 PM | |
| 4:48 PM | |
| 2:24 PM | |
| 12:00 PM | |
| 9:36 AM | |
| 7:12 AM | |
| 4:48 AM | |
| 2:24 AM | |
| 12:00 AM | |

Happy  Motivated  Anxious  Manic  Stable  Sad  Frustrated  Angry  Depressed  Tired

Becka's Best Publishing

# Self- Reflection:

Things you did today to achieve your goals: _____

_____

_____

_____

Things you did today that hindered your goals: _____

_____

_____

_____

Things that went well: _____

_____

_____

_____

Things that could have gone better: _____

_____

_____

_____

Notes: _____

_____

_____

_____

Becka's Best Publishing

Date: _____ Day: _____ Time: _____

Daily Goal: _____

To- Do List

○

○

○

○

Daily Habits

○ Drink Water

○ Personal Hygiene

○ Exercise

○ Meditate

○ Eat a healthy meal

## Sleep:

Quality: _____        Wake-Up: _____

Hours: _____            Bedtime: _____

## Chart your mood throughout the day:

Mood Chart

| 12:00 AM |
| 9:36 PM |
| 7:12 PM |
| 4:48 PM |
| 2:24 PM |
| 12:00 PM |
| 9:36 AM |
| 7:12 AM |
| 4:48 AM |
| 2:24 AM |
| 12:00 AM |

Happy  Motivated  Anxious  Manic  Stable  Sad  Frustrated  Angry  Depressed  Tired

Becka's Best Publishing

# Self- Reflection:

Things you did today to achieve your goals: _____

_____

_____

_____

Things you did today that hindered your goals: _____

_____

_____

_____

Things that went well: _____

_____

_____

_____

Things that could have gone better: _____

_____

_____

_____

Notes: _____

_____

_____

_____

Becka's Best Publishing

Date: _____ Day: _____ Time: _____

Daily Goal: _____

To- Do List

○

○

○

○

Daily Habits

- ○ Drink Water
- ○ Personal Hygiene
- ○ Exercise
- ○ Meditate
- ○ Eat a healthy meal

# Sleep:

Quality: _____    Wake-Up: _____

Hours: _____    Bedtime: _____

# Chart your mood throughout the day:

## Mood Chart

| Time | Happy | Motivated | Anxious | Manic | Stable | Sad | Frustrated | Angry | Depressed | Tired |
|------|-------|-----------|---------|-------|--------|-----|------------|-------|-----------|-------|
| 12:00 AM | | | | | | | | | | |
| 9:36 PM | | | | | | | | | | |
| 7:12 PM | | | | | | | | | | |
| 4:48 PM | | | | | | | | | | |
| 2:24 PM | | | | | | | | | | |
| 12:00 PM | | | | | | | | | | |
| 9:36 AM | | | | | | | | | | |
| 7:12 AM | | | | | | | | | | |
| 4:48 AM | | | | | | | | | | |
| 2:24 AM | | | | | | | | | | |
| 12:00 AM | | | | | | | | | | |

Becka's Best Publishing

# Self- Reflection:

Things you did today to achieve your goals: _____

_____

_____

_____

Things you did today that hindered your goals: _____

_____

_____

_____

Things that went well: _____

_____

_____

_____

Things that could have gone better: _____

_____

_____

_____

Notes: _____

_____

_____

_____

Becka's Best Publishing

Date: _____ Day: _____ Time: _____

## Daily Goal: _____

## To- Do List

○

○

○

○

## Daily Habits

○ Drink Water

○ Personal Hygiene

○ Exercise

○ Meditate

○ Eat a healthy meal

## Sleep:

Quality: _____          Wake-Up: _____

Hours: ____          Bedtime: _____

## Chart your mood throughout the day:

Mood Chart

| | Happy | Motivated | Anxious | Manic | Stable | Sad | Frustrated | Angry | Depressed | Tired |
|---|---|---|---|---|---|---|---|---|---|---|
| 12:00 AM | | | | | | | | | | |
| 9:36 PM | | | | | | | | | | |
| 7:12 PM | | | | | | | | | | |
| 4:48 PM | | | | | | | | | | |
| 2:24 PM | | | | | | | | | | |
| 12:00 PM | | | | | | | | | | |
| 9:36 AM | | | | | | | | | | |
| 7:12 AM | | | | | | | | | | |
| 4:48 AM | | | | | | | | | | |
| 2:24 AM | | | | | | | | | | |
| 12:00 AM | | | | | | | | | | |

Becka's Best Publishing

# Self- Reflection:

Things you did today to achieve your goals: _____

_____

_____

_____

Things you did today that hindered your goals: _____

_____

_____

_____

Things that went well: _____

_____

_____

_____

Things that could have gone better: _____

_____

_____

_____

Notes: _____

_____

_____

_____

Becka's Best Publishing

Date: _____ Day: _____ Time: _____

Daily Goal: _____

## To-Do List

- ○
- ○
- ○
- ○

## Daily Habits

- ○ Drink Water
- ○ Personal Hygiene
- ○ Exercise
- ○ Meditate
- ○ Eat a healthy meal

## Sleep:

Quality: _____      Wake-Up: _____

Hours: ____      Bedtime: _____

## Chart your mood throughout the day:

Mood Chart

| | Happy | Motivated | Anxious | Manic | Stable | Sad | Frustrated | Angry | Depressed | Tired |
|---|---|---|---|---|---|---|---|---|---|---|
| 12:00 AM | | | | | | | | | | |
| 9:36 PM | | | | | | | | | | |
| 7:12 PM | | | | | | | | | | |
| 4:48 PM | | | | | | | | | | |
| 2:24 PM | | | | | | | | | | |
| 12:00 PM | | | | | | | | | | |
| 9:36 AM | | | | | | | | | | |
| 7:12 AM | | | | | | | | | | |
| 4:48 AM | | | | | | | | | | |
| 2:24 AM | | | | | | | | | | |
| 12:00 AM | | | | | | | | | | |

Becka's Best Publishing

# Self- Reflection:

Things you did today to achieve your goals: _____

_____

_____

_____

Things you did today that hindered your goals: _____

_____

_____

_____

Things that went well: _____

_____

_____

_____

Things that could have gone better: _____

_____

_____

_____

Notes: _____

_____

_____

_____

Becka's Best Publishing

Date: _____ Day: _____ Time: _____

Daily Goal: _____

## To- Do List

- ○
- ○
- ○
- ○

## Daily Habits

- ○ Drink Water
- ○ Personal Hygiene
- ○ Exercise
- ○ Meditate
- ○ Eat a healthy meal

# Sleep:

Quality: _____          Wake-Up: _____

Hours: _____          Bedtime: _____

# Chart your mood throughout the day:

Mood Chart

|  |
|------|
| 12:00 AM |
| 9:36 PM |
| 7:12 PM |
| 4:48 PM |
| 2:24 PM |
| 12:00 PM |
| 9:36 AM |
| 7:12 AM |
| 4:48 AM |
| 2:24 AM |
| 12:00 AM |

Happy   Motivated   Anxious   Manic   Stable   Sad   Frustrated   Angry   Depressed   Tired

Becka's Best Publishing

# Self- Reflection:

Things you did today to achieve your goals: _____

_____

_____

_____

Things you did today that hindered your goals: _____

_____

_____

_____

Things that went well: _____

_____

_____

_____

Things that could have gone better: _____

_____

_____

_____

Notes: _____

_____

_____

_____

Becka's Best Publishing

Date: _____ Day: _____ Time: _____

Daily Goal: _____

## To- Do List

- ○
- ○
- ○
- ○

## Daily Habits

- ○ Drink Water
- ○ Personal Hygiene
- ○ Exercise
- ○ Meditate
- ○ Eat a healthy meal

## Sleep:

Quality: _____          Wake-Up; _____

Hours: _____          Bedtime: _____

## Chart your mood throughout the day:

Mood Chart

12:00 AM
9:36 PM
7:12 PM
4:48 PM
2:24 PM
12:00 PM
9:36 AM
7:12 AM
4:48 AM
2:24 AM
12:00 AM

Happy   Motivated   Anxious   Manic   Stable   Sad   Frustrated   Angry   Depressed   Tired

# Self- Reflection:

Things you did today to achieve your goals: _____
_____
_____
_____

Things you did today that hindered your goals: _____
_____
_____
_____

Things that went well: _____
_____
_____
_____

Things that could have gone better: _____
_____
_____
_____

Notes: _____
_____
_____
_____

Becka's Best Publishing

Date: _____ Day: _____ Time: _____

Daily Goal: _____

To- Do List

○

○

○

○

Daily Habits

○ Drink Water

○ Personal Hygiene

○ Exercise

○ Meditate

○ Eat a healthy meal

Sleep:

Quality: _____     Wake-Up: _____

Hours: _____     Bedtime: _____

Chart your mood throughout the day:

Mood Chart

|  | | |
|---|---|---|
| 12:00 AM | | |
| 9:36 PM | | |
| 7:12 PM | | |
| 4:48 PM | | |
| 2:24 PM | | |
| 12:00 PM | | |
| 9:36 AM | | |
| 7:12 AM | | |
| 4:48 AM | | |
| 2:24 AM | | |
| 12:00 AM | | |

Happy  Motivated  Anxious  Manic  Stable  Sad  Frustrated  Angry  Depressed  Tired

Becka's Best Publishing

# Self- Reflection:

Things you did today to achieve your goals: _____

_____

_____

_____

Things you did today that hindered your goals: _____

_____

_____

_____

Things that went well: _____

_____

_____

_____

Things that could have gone better: _____

_____

_____

_____

Notes: _____

_____

_____

_____

Becka's Best Publishing

Date: _____ Day: _____ Time: _____

## Daily Goal: _____

### To- Do List

○

○

○

○

### Daily Habits

○ Drink Water

○ Personal Hygiene

○ Exercise

○ Meditate

○ Eat a healthy meal

## Sleep:

Quality: _____          Wake-Up: _____

Hours: _____          Bedtime: _____

## Chart your mood throughout the day:

Mood Chart

| | Happy | Motivated | Anxious | Manic | Stable | Sad | Frustrated | Angry | Depressed | Tired |
|---|---|---|---|---|---|---|---|---|---|---|
| 12:00 AM | | | | | | | | | | |
| 9:36 PM | | | | | | | | | | |
| 7:12 PM | | | | | | | | | | |
| 4:48 PM | | | | | | | | | | |
| 2:24 PM | | | | | | | | | | |
| 12:00 PM | | | | | | | | | | |
| 9:36 AM | | | | | | | | | | |
| 7:12 AM | | | | | | | | | | |
| 4:48 AM | | | | | | | | | | |
| 2:24 AM | | | | | | | | | | |
| 12:00 AM | | | | | | | | | | |

Becka's Best Publishing

# Self- Reflection:

Things you did today to achieve your goals: _____

_____

_____

_____

Things you did today that hindered your goals: _____

_____

_____

_____

Things that went well: _____

_____

_____

_____

Things that could have gone better: _____

_____

_____

_____

Notes: _____

_____

_____

_____

Becka's Best Publishing

# Coping Skills

Now that you have mastered 90 days of reaching for your goals, recording your moods, and reflecting on these events, symptoms, and behaviors, do you feel stronger? Braver? More confident?_____

_____

_____

_____

_____

What skills or habits did you develop that made things easier or better? What skills or habits would you like to develop?_____

_____

_____

_____

_____

_____

_____

Becka's Best Publishing

# Coping Ideas

You are not powerless, Bipolar can be mastered. It takes time, patience and discipline, but with the right coping mechanisms you, too, can live a happy and fruitful life.

The first thing you can do is get involved. Explore all the resources available to you and come up with a plan of attack. Don't continue to let yourself be railroaded by Bipolar, learn about it instead.

Be Patient.

Take your meds as directed.

Continue to work with your doctor until you find the right medications for you. This may take some time.

Heal. Whether through therapy or alternative methods, learn about healing yourself, letting go of the past, and forgiveness.

Be selfish. It's okay to put yourself first. Having a bad day? That's okay, go home and take care of yourself, hopefully tomorrow will be better.

Rest, Relax. Breathe.

Monitor your mood and symptoms and identify your triggers/stressors.

Develop your wellness toolbox. Do things you like. Hobbies. Activities. People. Places.

Develop positive daily habits.

Becka's Best Publishing

# Journal Review

You did it! You are now 3 months closer to your next goal. Take a moment to review the last 3 months. What did you learn? What do you still struggle? What is something new you will try going forward?

_____

_____

_____

_____

_____

_____

_____

_____

_____

_____

_____

_____

_____

_____

_____

_____

_____

Becka's Best Publishing

# Helpful Resources

## YouTube:

Polar Warriors

Awareness – Dr. Robert McKeon

## Reddit:

r/bipolar

r/bipolar2

## Facebook:

Women's Bipolar & Anxiety Support Group

Mental Health Support Group Warriors

## Online:

Substance Abuse and Mental Health Services Administration

www.samhsa.gov/

National Help Hotline – 1-800-622-4357 (HELP)

National Alliance on Mental Illness

www.nami.org/

Help Hotline – 800-950-NAMI

info@nami.org

Text "NAMI" to 741741

Mental Health America

www.mentalhealthamerica.net/

1-800-273-TALK

Text "MHA" to 741741

## Suicide:

Hotline – 1-800-273-8255

## Relationships:

Stephan Speaks with Lewis Howes (YouTube)

## Career:

Tony Robbins – Any of his stuff for any reason!

Ken Coleman – Ramsey Solutions

## Finance:

Dave Ramsey – Ramsey Solutions

## Books:

The Bipolar Disorder Workbook – Peter Forster, MD

The Bipolar Disorder Survival Guide – David J. Miklowitz, PHD

Two Bipolar Chicks Guide To Survival: Tips for Living with Bipolar Disorder – Wendy K Williamson & Honora Rose

OMG That's Me!: Bipolar Disorder, Depression, Anxiety, Panic Attacks, and More. – Dave Mowry

Becka's Best Publishing

# Glossary:

ANTIDEPRESSANT: Medication used to treat depression and other mood and anxiety disorders.

ANTIPSYCHOTIC: Medication used to treat psychosis.

AUDITORY HALLUCINATIONS: Hearing something that is not real. Hearing voices is an example of auditory hallucinations.

BIPOLAR DISORDER: A disorder that causes severe and unusually high and low shifts in mood, energy, and activity levels as well as unusual shifts in the ability to carry out day-to-day tasks. (Also known as Manic Depression)

CBT: Cognitive Behavioral Therapy in which a person focuses on solving current problems through behavior patterns.

CBT-P: Cognitive Behavioral Therapy for Psychosis, in which a person uses behavior patterns to address symptoms of psychosis. (i.e. hearing voices)

CHRONIC: Persisting for a long time or constantly recurring.

DEPRESSIVE: Emotional state of being down, sad, tired, fatigued, demotivated, having trouble sleeping, and more.

EPISODE: A bout of depression or mania lasting 3 days or more.

Becka's Best Publishing

MANIA: Emotional state of being energetic, happy, euphoric, excited, agitated, wired, motivated, and a bit reckless.

PSYCHOSIS: Condition that affects the mind.

DELUSIONS: Beliefs that have no basis in reality.

DUAL DIAGNOSIS: Having a mental health disorder in addition to a drug or alcohol addiction.

HALLUCINATIONS: Hearing, seeing, touching, smelling or tasting things that are not real.

MANIA: An abnormally elevated or irritable mood. Associated with bipolar disorder.

MOOD DISORDERS: Mental disorders primarily affecting a person's mood.

PSYCHOTHERAPY: Treatment of mental illness by talking about problems rather than by using medication based on CBT principles and emphasizes resilience training, illness and wellness management, and coping skills.

SCHIZOAFFECTIVE DISORDER: A mental condition that causes both a loss of contact with reality (psychosis) and mood problems (depression or mania).

SCHIZOPHRENIA: A severe mental disorder that appears in late adolescence or early adulthood. People with schizophrenia may have hallucinations, delusions, loss of personality, confusion, agitation, social withdrawal, psychosis and/or extremely odd behavior.

Becka's Best Publishing

# About the Author

Hello, it's nice to meet you. My name is Becka Yaeger and I sincerely hope you enjoyed this journal. Bipolar manifests for everyone in different ways and it is my mission to help people cope with that the best way they can.

I decided to create this journal because in my pursuit to understand my own Bipolar I was having a hard time organizing all my thoughts and relevant data in one spot. Most other journals are really just planners and they are marketed toward being more "positive" and "grateful". Granted, I am not against those mindsets, they weren't allowing me to think about my condition in the way that I needed.

That's the thing about Bipolar, you can't just think the condition away. No amount of positive thinking and mental strength is going to cure you of Bipolar, so I got practical.

I have big dreams and goals. I want to get into the self-publishing business for fiction writers, I want to offer premium proofreading, editing, marketing, and consulting to authors. I want to learn copywriting for commercial clients, I want to live my life my way.

I designed this journal with those goals in mind. I've been chasing after a life I just can't seem to grab on to and decided that I needed to really ask myself, "What do I need to get that done?"

My answer was a journal that would keep me on task and looking forward.

# Becka's Best Publishing

Becka's Best is exactly what it sounds like, the very best I have to offer:

Becka's Best Publishing – Guides, Journals, Novels, and other content published by me, Becka Yaeger.

Becka's Best Editorial Services – Beta Critiques, Proofreading, and Copyediting

Becka's Best Marketing – Copywriting and Social Media Management

## Contact:

Becka Yaeger

becka@beckasbest.com

www.beckasbest.com/

@beckasbestproofreading (Instagram)

Please feel free to send me any feedback or suggestions for future journal ideas and concepts. I would love to hear from you. Tell me your success stories or your failures. I guarantee a personal response back within 24 hours.

Take care of yourself. Love, Becka

Made in the USA
Monee, IL
17 May 2020